CONTEMPORARY
DOORWAYS

CONTEMPORARY DOORWAYS

ARCHITECTURAL ENTRANCES, TRANSITIONS AND THRESHOLDS

CATHERINE SLESSOR

MITCHELL BEAZLEY

CONTEMPORARY DOORWAYS

Catherine Slessor

Copyright © Octopus Publishing Group Ltd 2002

First published in Great Britain in 2002 by Mitchell Beazley,
an imprint of Octopus Publishing Group Ltd,
2–4 Heron Quays, Docklands, London E14 4JP

Commissioning Editor **Mark Fletcher**
Executive Editor **Hannah Barnes-Murphy**
Art Director **Vivienne Brar**
Project Editor **Virginia McLeod**
Editor **Penny Warren**
Designer **Colin Goody**
Production **Alex Wiltshire**
Picture Research **Helen Stallion**
Proof Reader **Joan Porter**
Indexer **Richard Bird**

A CIP catalogue record for this book is
available from the British Library

ISBN 1 84000 509 2

Set in Trade Gothic and AvantGarde
Produced by Toppan Printing Co., (HK) Ltd.
Printed and bound in China

front cover *Comme des Garçons store, New York City,
by Future Systems. Photograph © Richard Davies*

back cover *Timber pivoting door, by Yturbe Arquitectos.
Photograph © Cecelia Innes /The Interior Archive*

title page *Entrance canopy to the Portugese Pavilion,
Expo 2000, Hanover, Germany by Alvaro Siza.
Photograph © Peter Mackinven /VIEW*

contents page *Conference room door, Tindall Riley & Co.,
New City Court, London, by Fletcher Priest Architects.
Photograph © Chris Gascoigne /VIEW*

CONTENTS

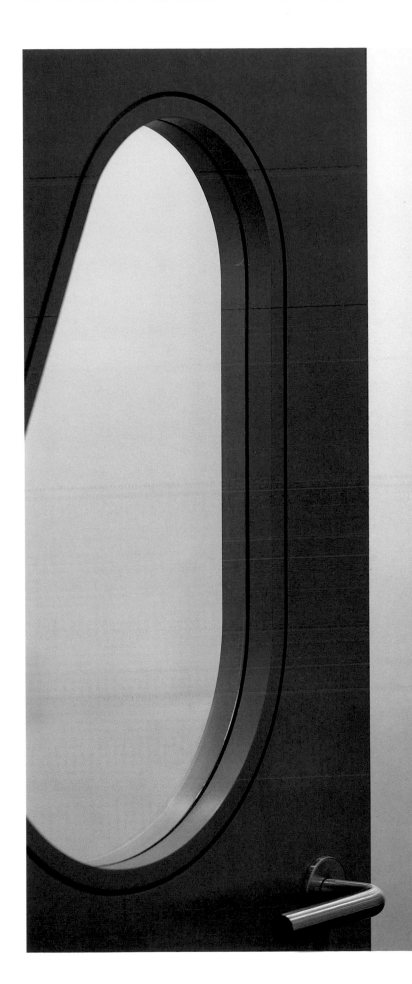

THE DOORWAY: A HISTORY

A door is a door is a door. Or is it? Could there be something more to entrances than the functional division of space? From time immemorial, the door has acted as the boundary of mankind's protected and secure sources of food, shelter and warmth. Beyond lies the outside world, with its unknown dangers. Every door is at once a boundary, shutting off one area from another, yet it is also a connection between outside and inside. Part of the mystique of doorways is that they are in-between places – where the inside and outside worlds come together, where private and public meet, where the known and unknown conjoin. The unexpected knock at the door can change lives forever.

right *The Pantheon in Rome, the "temple of all gods" built between 27 and 25BC. A massive pedimented portico encloses and marks the entrance. Remarkably, its original bronze doors still survive.*

The many styles of door evolved by different cultures reflect the concerns of society over time. The massive gates of Indian cities (made of huge crossed wooden beams studded with giant iron spikes) were designed to withstand the charge of war elephants, for instance. By contrast, the *shoji* doors of traditional Japanese architecture (made of delicately thin rice paper) were designed to diffuse daylight and create a soft translucence. The curtain of wooden beads used as a passageway door in Mediterranean countries gives a degree of visual privacy, but allows and encourages conversations between relatives and friends. In the Netherlands, farmhouse doors have top sections that can be opened to let in light and air, while keeping out straying livestock.

Throughout history, the design and embellishment of doors have reached extraordinary heights of invention and sophistication. The entrances to French Gothic cathedrals, which are masterpieces of carved stone, wood and ornamental ironwork, are one such example. Some of the fabled gold and silver doors of ancient Persian mosques still exist, a reminder of the importance that people placed on their spiritual life. For many centuries, the nomadic tribes of the Hindu Kush mountains have woven intricate tapestries that form the entrances to their tents. Though inevitably less enduring than stone, wooden or metal doors, they too have come to be regarded as great works of art.

In architecture of almost all types and periods, particular attention has been devoted to the doorway and the crossing of a threshold can have symbolic and even religious significance. In mythological terms, the door represents hope, opportunity, opening and the entrance to a new life, initiation and shelter. Perhaps, most profoundly, it epitomizes passage from one state or world to another. Doors and gates mark the threshold between the profane and sacred, natural and super-natural, the living and the dead, and often such portals are guarded by fabulous beasts and monsters. Art and literature abound with images of doors and entrances and legends of guardians, gatekeepers and rites of passage, from *Alice's Adventures in Wonderland*, in which doors are a recurring metaphor for an exploration of the subconscious, to Milton's apocalyptic description of the Gates of Hell in *Paradise Lost*, "On a sudden open fly; With impetuous recoil and jarring sound; The infernal doors, and on their hinges grate; Harsh thunder."

right *Traditional Japanese* shoji *screens diffuse daylight through translucent membranes of rice paper which are stretched over gridded wooden frames. The sliding doors open up to extend the interior space and frame views.*

below *An Indian tepee, with its entrance protected by a flap of animal skin. Nomadic tribes often dignify the entrances to their tents with decorated panels or intricately woven cloth.*

An open door symbolizes opportunity and liberation. In the Bible, Christ proclaims "I am the door" (John 10:9) and the Virgin Mary symbolizes the Gate of Heaven. The three doors of a cathedral or church signify faith, hope and charity. A closed door represents the Fall – the expulsion of Adam and Eve from the Garden of Eden. In Hindu temples, gods and goddesses are carved on door jambs, indicating the deity through whom man enters the presence of the divine. In Roman mythology, Janus is the god of the doorway, and holds the keys to the power of opening and closing. In the Zodiac, the summer solstice in Cancer is "the door of men" and symbolizes the dying power and descent of the sun. The winter solstice in Capricorn is the "door of the gods", representing the ascent and rising power of the sun. In parts of the Far East, the practice of *feng shui*, a form of geomancy, still exerts a strong influence on architecture. Doors and openings must be positioned so as to promote harmony and the flow of *chi* or vital energy to ward off evil spirits.

Language also yields clues to the importance attached to doorways. In Latin, the word for door (*fores*) came to be associated with the distinction between public and private domains. The term *foris* or *forum* referred to a public space outside the door. Phrases

below *Hell's Mouth (Sacro Bosco) in Bomarzo. A sixteenth-century Italian garden grotto is enclosed by a giant, grotesque mask that is emblematic of the doorway as a transition and threshold into an unknown realm.*

above *A Roman temple carved into the rose-red rock cliffs of the Arabian desert. Here the door is a gateway to the realm of the sacred.*

such as "behind closed doors" or "to show someone the door" bear witness to this view of the door as a junction between public and private space, and as an embodiment of the powers of inclusion and exclusion.

In their functional, visual and symbolic roles, doors (and windows) constitute the essential architectural language through which a building can be read and interpreted. The position, proportion, materials and decoration of openings give important clues to the building's role, status and historical context. The character of a façade can be transformed by treatment of its openings. The play of light on a deeply recessed doorway or projecting bay window can be used to articulate the wall surface and emphasize particular aspects of the building, such as its entrance or main storey.

Like many building elements, the door has undergone a fascinating process of evolution. Primitive tribes always kept access openings to the smallest possible dimension in order to deter intruders and wild animals and they often rolled boulders across the mouths of caves as barriers. As living patterns changed and a less hazardous and more structured social order developed, a mobile framework would usually be placed over the doorway. Doors from this period were not hung on hinges and were assembled from a variety of materials, ranging from wattle-work to animal skins stretched over a wooden frame.

The history of early doorways is recorded in the detail of the doors they framed. In classical antiquity, certain formal and constructional principles were established. The Roman architect Vitruvius, who composed the first study of architecture and gave it an ordered, intellectual foundation, codified certain rules for the design, proportion and placement of doors. Book IV of Vitruvius's great treatise, *The Ten Books of Architecture*, provides detailed instructions for temple doorways and the appearance of general-purpose Doric or Ionic doors.

The form of early doorways reflected available building materials and construction techniques. As a general principle, the beam or lintel had to be sufficiently strong to take the weight of the wall above it and transfer it to the side openings. Since wood has the right kind of elastic strength to perform this task efficiently, most early lintels were made of timber, but these could span only a limited distance. The need to restrict the span of the lintel together with the shape of the human figure established the vertical proportions of Greek and Roman doors. Even when stone was used, the same design principles were adopted. In common with many doors of antiquity, the doorway of the Parthenon in Athens, dating from 438BC, tapers in width to reduce the span of the lintel. Doorposts and beam are expressed, with the ends of the lintel projecting into the wall. The edges of the door are emphasized by a simple moulding.

The huge doorway of the Pantheon in Rome, with its original bronze doors, is a remarkable survival from the second century AD. However, although the mouldings and decoration follow a conventional pattern, there is no reduction in width at the top of the door. Inside this opening is a pair of Doric pilasters that support their own architrave or inner lintel. Above this inner architrave is a large window, or fanlight, in its own frame. A monumental portico emphasizes the main entrance. The elaboration of a door with a portico, sweeping stairway or triumphal arch gives special, sometimes ceremonial significance to the threshold as a symbol of transition. Both portico and porch (ancestors of the *pronaos* of a Greek temple), also have the obvious function of protecting against the elements. The use of door surrounds and porches to give added importance to doors was a widespread Roman practice and marks the beginning of the embellishment of doorways.

During the Middle Ages, the power of the Church triumphant and a move away from the prevailing obsession with grimmer aspects of sin, guilt and death gave rise to the grandeur of Gothic cathedrals. Elaborate stone carvings and decoration of church doors and entrances served to remind believers of the perils of this world and the rewards of the next, as well as emphasizing the transition from profane to sacred ground. "This is the House of God and the Gate of Heaven," says the psalmist in the liturgy for the consecration of a church. Amiens Cathedral, dating from the thirteenth century, had at least nine entrances differentiated in form, size and function. The façades in which these portals were set served as the backdrop for various sorts of events. The space in front of

left *The Gates of Paradise, Lorenzo Ghiberti's bronze doors on the Baptistery in Florence illustrate scenes from lives of Old Testament figures and is one of the finest achievements of the Renaissance.*

above *St Mark's Basilica in Venice is richly adorned with carvings, mosaics and sculptures to bring the word of God to an illiterate populace. The central portal is framed by some of Italy's finest Byzantine carvings.*

13

the main portal, for instance, was used for burials. It was also a place where people might seek asylum, where oaths were taken and the law was administered. The richly decorated entrances in the north front served as bridal portals where wedding rings were exchanged before marriage ceremonies. Church doors also marked the boundary between life and the hereafter. The path to heaven led through the church portal and this message was powerfully conveyed to an illiterate populace by means of sculptural imagery.

A powerful example of this dissemination can be seen in the set of ornate doors made for the ancient Baptistery in Florence. Designed by Lorenzo Ghiberti, the cast-bronze doors were added to the east side of the building in 1452 and represent one of the earliest and most powerful works of the Renaissance. The Baptistery itself dates back to the fourth century and the new doors were commissioned in 1401 to mark Florence's deliverance from an all-consuming plague. Each of the ten panels illustrates incidents from the lives of an Old Testament figure and each square is totally gilded, so that the scenes appear bathed in a radiant golden light. Perspective is used to create a highly convincing illusion of depth, enhanced by the use of gold. Michelangelo called them the "Gates of Paradise", punning on the Italian term *paradiso*, which was the area between a baptistery and the entrance to its cathedral, and onto which the doors open.

Ghiberti's doors were strongly influenced by the humanist and artistic theories of Leon Battista Alberti, whose architectural ideas and notions of the construction and organization of pictorial space shaped Renaissance thought. Seeking to make a moral and formal case for the principles of classicism first evolved by Vitruvius, Alberti defined a series of terms according to which architecture may be translated into practice. These included the opening (*apertio*), which constituted all manner of entrances and exits for sunlight, air, waste, water, people and objects. Unlike any other architectural writer before or after, Alberti assembled and generalized these elements under the heading of *apertio*.

Alberti's theories were put into practice by many architects, notably Andrea Palladio, who distilled the essence of classicism from Vitruvian rules and ancient models. His buildings are mainly secular, reflecting the new importance of secular rather than religious commissions that came to dominate architecture from

left *The monumental doorway of the Natural History Museum in London, was designed by Alfred Waterhouse. Victorian secular buildings often appropriated the forms of church architecture to create an imposing aura. Reflecting the building's function, the doorway is embellished with terracotta flora and fauna.*

right *A Georgian six-panelled door, the most common domestic door type of the eighteenth century. The plain door is surrounded by an elaborate doorcase and surmounted by a fanlight to bring light into the entrance hall beyond.*

the sixteenth century onwards. Palladio designed many grand villas, such as the Villa Chiericati near Vicenza in northern Italy, which has an entrance portico so large that it forms the only significant element of the design. Palladio recognized the importance of such elements and praised their usefulness as a means to convey dignity. "In all villas and some townhouses I placed a frontispiece on the front façade where the main entrances are situated, for such frontispieces denote the entrance to the house and greatly contribute to the grandeur and splendour of the work."

As Palladio observed, in houses, as with civic buildings, the entrance forms the focus of the composition. The design and construction of the domestic doorway also provided a guide to the wealth and status of the household. Until around 1700, the majority of houses had a simple planked front door, typically lengths of oak with supporting braces or ledges nailed across their backs. In the case of manor houses, castles and other large buildings, panelled doors imparted a sense of grandeur, but their use was rare. After 1700, however, the more complex panelled door became the dominant form, comprising an arrangement of stiles and rails – respectively vertical and horizontal members –

below *The iconic Villa Savoie by Le Corbusier, a white concrete box elevated on pilotis.* One of the earliest houses of the Modern Movement (built in 1931), it embodies a fluid plan and streamlined forms. Placed on the ground floor, the main entrance does not make a grandiose statement.

above *The Schröder House in Utrecht (1924) designed by Gerrit Rietveld, a cubist composition of smooth planes articulated by primary colours. The door forms part of this abstract collage.*

surrounding an arrangement of flat panels. The design and proportion of the panels changed, until by the late-eighteenth century, six-panelled doors were the most common type of door. This historic model is still to be seen gracing many houses, including the British Prime Minister's residence at 10 Downing Street, possibly the most famous front door in the world.

The grandest Georgian doors were made from seasoned oak or West Indian mahogany. In less wealthy households, inferior oak or softwoods were used, painted a single dark colour. While the body of the Georgian door was usually quite plain, with sober and unobtrusive mouldings, great exuberance was often exhibited in the adjacent doorcase and fanlight. Doorcases took the form of columns or pilasters supporting ornate hoods, cornices, pediments or canopies. Fanlights first appeared in around 1720. Designed to light dark hallways, they became increasingly elaborate. The introduction of slim iron glazing bars in the 1780s gave rise to delicate cobweb patterns of iron tracery and glass.

Many of the now familiar door fittings were comparatively recent developments. Locks remained fairly primitive until the mid-nineteenth century when use of the rotating Yale lock (patented in 1848) became widespread. Letter boxes and the numbering of doors were also mid-nineteenth century developments, in response to the introduction of the Penny Post, when letters were no longer paid for by the recipient. Door knockers date from the seventeenth century, and were originally simple variations on a ring handle executed in wrought iron or brass. The S-shaped knocker, known as the "doctor's knocker", was introduced during the Georgian period and changed little until the nineteenth century. Victorians favoured animal or classical themes for their door knockers, such as eagles, lions, Medusa's head or a shield embellished with a family coat-of-arms.

By the mid-nineteenth century, the six-panelled door gave way to a simpler four-panelled design, with two large panels surmounting two smaller ones. Frosted or stained glass was often substituted for the wood of the two upper panels. These developments were made possible by the great advances made in glass technology; in 1832, for instance, Continental-style plate glass was introduced into Britain, enabling the production of larger panes. The increasing sophistication and reliability of nineteenth-century glass enhanced the potential for colour and decoration. The last great age of domestic door

design came with the inter-war period, when stylized motifs and the imaginative use of plain or stained glass made it possible to produce the familiar suburban door.

In the first half of the twentieth century, Modernist architects were eager to strip away the clutter of superfluous ornament and doorways became decidedly less prominent. At Le Corbusier's Villa Savoie, for instance, the entrance, tucked away under the prominent overhanging upper storey, barely registers. And at Gerrit Rietveld's Schröder House in Utrecht, the door forms part of an abstract collage of flat planes. As Modernist conceptions of space evolved and plans became more fluid, the grand, centralized entrance has became less important. Another legacy of the late nineteenth century was the revolving door, first credited to T. Van Kannel, an American manufacturer. Yet today's

modern derivatives bear little resemblance to the original elegant mahogany and bevelled glass assemblies that liveried hotel or shop doormen would discreetly revolve on the approach of customers. Revolving doors possess certain advantages over conventional hinged doors, such as the reduction of noise, and the prevention of pollution through dust and rain. They reached their zenith during the era of the Edwardian steamship, where their luxury and opulence were emulated on shore in commercial and civic buildings from department stores to art galleries. Most modern revolving doors are automatically controlled and the most striking designs, such as Foster & Partners' doors at Stansted Airport or Richard Rogers' Lloyds' Building in London embody an enviable sleekness and seamlessness.

As the following case studies show, the importance of the doorway remains undiminished, and it continues to be celebrated with great ingenuity and imagination by contemporary architects around the world. From a simple French house to the monumental portico of the new Reichstag, from a Japanese bathroom to a New York boutique, doors retain the power to communicate and embrace, to protect and hide. Imbued with symbolic and historical significance, the doorway remains one of architecture's most compelling and enduringly fascinating elements.

ECLECTIC ENTRANCES

As the focus of façades, doors can be simple or ornate, inviting or repelling, but whatever their character or context, they are never insignificant. In their myriad forms – swinging, sliding, side-hinged, revolving, folding, louvre doors, flush doors, French doors, Dutch doors – they are chameleons, changing their appearance to suit circumstances and a multiplicity of uses. This chapter considers the extravagant and the eclectic, where the humble doorway assumes an astonishing range of guises, from Ushida Findlay's sensuous fur-clad bathroom door in a Japanese house, to Francis Soler's Parisian apartments, featuring sliding doors embellished with translucent coloured images to create a series of framed kinetic sequences. Through the power of architectural imagination, the doorway transcends its basic function and is elevated to a work of art.

right *Doors can assume a rich variety of disguises – even an apparently simple entrance, such as this one to a shopping centre car park in Reykjavik, Iceland, by Studio Granda, embodies a striking contrast of materials.*

ENGELEN MOORE
PRICE O'REILLY HOUSE, SYDNEY, 1995

Engelen Moore was given an unusual brief: to create a house that would double as a photographic studio. The result was this deceptively simple building, which is located in a suburban Sydney street lined with terraced houses, flats and warehouses. It occupies the site of two terraced houses and local planning guidelines stipulated that the street side of the building should reflect the previous domestic scale, rather than that of the warehouses. As a result, the two-storey street elevation is divided both vertically and horizontally into two bays, with the garage and front door of the house dominating the ground floor. The major horizontal elements align with the adjoining terraced houses and each bay also relates proportionately to them. The entrance and garage doors are clad in sleek panels of composite aluminium sheeting. Unusually, the entrance door is 3.3m (9¾ft) high (i.e. around 1m or 3¼ft higher than a conventional door), its scale dictated by the subdivision of the façade. The upper level of the street frontage is clad in extruded aluminium louvres which can be opened completely to allow light and cooling breezes to enter, or closed to form an opaque skin.

Economy was one of the main design criteria; the other was the need to make a big space that could be used both as a photographic studio and as a living area. This big volume – indeed the whole house – has been created in an almost industrial way with steel portal frames 6m (19½ft) high and 7m (23ft) wide, blockwork side walls and compressed fibre boards on front and back parapets. The entire shell has been painted white, forming a crisp, cubic volume.

The most dramatic element of the house is the rear wall. This is composed of six glass panels, each 6m (19½ft) high. They are held in slim metal frames and can be slid and stacked, like a set of huge folding doors, so that the interior may be opened up to a courtyard (with a small pool) and the sky. In summer, natural through ventilation can be achieved by opening up the sliding doors and the louvres on the street side. The glass wall, which in summer is shaded by a large eucalyptus tree in a neighbouring garden, allows solar penetration during winter to warm up the house, and the thermal mass of the blockwork walls retains the heat.

Because the big space has to be rapidly and easily converted from living room to studio, the architects devised special lightweight, wheeled furniture that can be arranged as needs dictate. A striking triumph of lightness and simplicity, the house/studio embodies a practical yet highly sensual modern lifestyle.

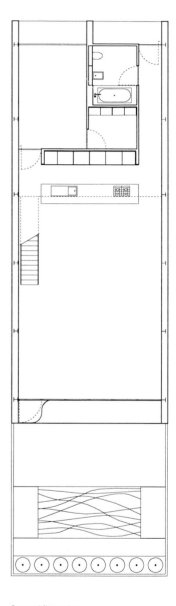

Ground floor plan

right *The dramatic garden elevation is made up of metal framed glass panels that slide and stack like huge folding doors to reveal the airy volume of the living space within.*

left *The entire living space; kitchen, dining and sitting area are opened up to the tiny garden, where a tree "borrowed" from a neighbour provides welcome shade. A deep plunge pool is cut into the ground along the rear garden wall.*

above left *From the exterior, the double-height volume of the living area is emphasized by the stark white portal frame surrounding the opening. The doors are guided in tracks cut into the floor and ceiling, and stack unobtrusively to one side.*

above right *The hermetic street frontage follows the geometry of the neighbouring Victorian terraced houses. Entrance and garage doors are clad in sleek aluminium sheeting, while aluminium louvres can be opened up on the upper floor to encourage cross-ventilation.*

Plan of entry and glass bridge

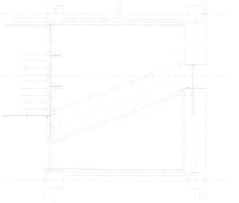

above *Looking from the ground floor, up through the entry space to the sky above, the steel-and-glass bridge demonstrates the geometrical complexity and stark contrasts between light and shade that characterize this unusual house.*

KENGO KUMA
GLASS HOUSE, ATAMI, 1995

Perched on a hillside overlooking the bay of Atami, south of Tokyo, this remarkable three-storey villa seems suspended between earth and sky. Effortlessly manipulating glass and water, Kengo Kuma has created an abstract architecture that depends for its effect on the changing qualities of light and reflection. At times, the boundary between the material and the insubstantial seems to dissolve. Entry is at intermediate level through a garage and an open door set in an imposing granite wall, which leads to a steel-and-glass bridge spanning a pool below. The delicate, ethereal quality of the bridge heightens the vertiginous drama of the entry sequence. Protected from the elements by a steel-and-glass canopy, the bridge crosses an open void to connect with a staircase that links the various levels of the house. Kuma believes that the life that unfolds in buildings is just as important as their architecture, so internal circulation routes are contrived to incite the greatest possible interest.

On the lower two levels, the main elements of the house are arranged around a central core. Rooms to the south and east are enclosed by glass walls, with private quarters and bathrooms screened off. The climax of the composition is on the top floor, where the house is surmounted by an impossibly insubstantial glass pavilion. Detached from the main part of the building by a glass walkway, this diaphanous structure floats on a sheet of water under a glass canopy screened by silver louvres. From the transparent pavilion, which is used for dining, spectacular views of the bay are framed by beams and columns. These vistas are tempered by the faint reflections of the glass membrane and by light percolating through the louvres onto the lustrous surface of the surrounding pool.

Kuma's architecture experiments with the very act of seeing. The house at Atami is defined not as an object, but as a diversity of spaces resulting from the imposition of transparent planes on the landscape. Elements, such as the sheet of water, which melds with the sea beyond, are treated as filters, or abstract frames, rather than solid, earthbound obstacles. Far from being introverted, the house opens up to become part of the landscape.

right *The imposing stone mass of the building is contrasted with the lightness of the horizontally cantilevered planes that mark the entrance.*

DALY GENIK
TARZANA RESIDENCE, SAN DIEGO, 1999

Set on the edge of a citrus and avocado ranch in North San Diego county, this unusual dwelling replaces a ranch house destroyed in a bush fire. The client, a second-generation citrus rancher, wanted a building that would serve as a guest house for holiday visits from his grown-up daughters and their families. A remote area in the foothills of Mount Palomar was chosen for its western orientation and steep topography, which helps to prevent frost damage to the fruit trees. Covered with exposed granite boulders, underlying granite monoliths and decomposed granite shale, the site has a craggy, primeval quality.

The single-storey house has two slightly splayed wings of sleeping quarters flanking a central living and dining room. Their geometry forms a west-facing courtyard with sweeping views of orange groves and the coast beyond. A swimming pool notches into one side of the courtyard. The external treatment of the house explores a finely honed language of layering, with metal and concrete panels alternately veiling and revealing inner glass boxes. This has an important practical dimension: the outer panels shield the glass from wind-driven embers, so protecting the house from bush fires. Presenting a hermetic face to the surrounding landscape, the outer wall of the two bedroom wings is sheathed in a corrugated concrete skin, incised with horizontal glazed slits. On the courtyard side, full-height panels made of perforated aluminium fold out crisply, like a concertina, to open up the house. A similar system is used on the main living and dining block, except the aluminium panels slide up vertically, like garage doors, projecting to create areas of shade. In winter, the panels can be used to reflect light onto the living room ceiling. Opaque during the day, the perforated screens have a seductive, gauzy translucence after dark, as light diffuses through the fine mesh.

Interior finishes extend the theme of simple, tectonic lucidity. Walls and ceilings are clad in smooth birch plywood; floors in polished concrete and linoleum. Sliding timber panels in vivid hues enclose the bedrooms, adding colour and animation. Daly Genik's preoccupation with lightness, modular planning, prefabrication and nature draws on and extends the industrially inspired traditions of Californian Modernism, and in this project these qualities clearly find resonant expression.

left *With the perforated aluminium panel open, the house reveals itself to the landscape, and provides a lively architectural rhythm to the façade.*

Site plan

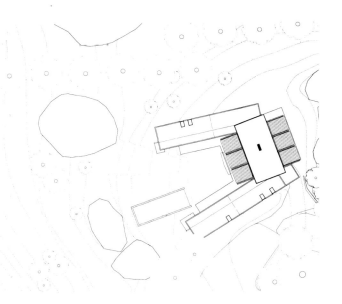

29

above left and right *At night the panels glow with the warm diffused light coming from the interior. From inside, the courtyard and pool are still visible through the protective metal barrier.*

right *Vertical panels lift up from the façade of the main living spaces, shading them from the rigours of the harsh Californian sun.*

FUTURE SYSTEMS
PROJECT 222, PEMBROKESHIRE, 1999

Bunkered in a hillside overlooking a bay, this holiday house on the remote Pembrokeshire coast resembles a prehistoric burial mound. Future Systems, who designed the project, treated the site, which lies in a National Park, with extreme sensitivity and discretion. The beauty and drama of the remote surroundings – the house sits on top of a cliff with stunning vistas over the bay – inspired Future Systems to design a building that sits lightly on the ground, emphasizing the quality of the interior spaces and the views.

Adopting an organic, structurally strong form, the house is partially buried in the site, becoming an almost invisible part of the landscape. The pod-like structure was inserted into a sloping cleft which is turfed and planted with local grasses and flowers. A concrete slab

and retaining wall support a stressed-skin plywood roof, complete with membrane and turf. When the planting matures, the building will look even less conspicuous, like a wartime bunker or romantic ruin. The only clues to its presence will be its full-height glazed entrance, the elliptical glass façade which looks like a lens or eye incised into the cliff, and the chimney of the woodburning stove, which projects above ground like a periscope.

Framed by bunkers of earth, the main entrance lies to the rear of the house and the eventual intention is to obscure the entryway with trees. The door is a simple glazed panel set in the diaphanous walls. Identical doors are placed along the main façade, so that the interior spaces can be opened up in warm weather. The openable portholes in the glazing, which are products normally used in boats, are an example of Future Systems' ingenious adaptation of products and construction technologies from other fields.

The brilliant yellow of the interior echoes the vivid gorse bushes in the surrounding landscape. Within, the arrangement is simple, with a bedroom at each end screened and separated from the central living area by teardrop-shaped bathroom pods, one of which incorporates a kitchen along its curved edge. The pods stop short of the ceiling so as not to disrupt the volume and play of light. Despite the house's apparent fragility, its double-glazed walls and earth bunkers help it to retain heat in winter and to keep cool in summer.

above *The glass entry door, provides a subtle transition from the stark modernity of the interior to the rugged Pembrokeshire landscape.*

right *The porthole windows allow fresh air to circulate through the house despite the sometimes harsh coastal weather. On calmer days, the glazed doors can be opened up to the sea.*

Axonometric

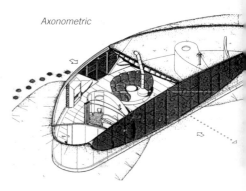

JACQUES MOUSSAFIR
PRIVATE RESIDENCE, SURENNES, 1998

This house in the suburbs of Surennes is an enigmatic composition of translucent, transparent and opaque planes. Economically planned over two storeys and enclosing a small garden, the solid character of the lower level contrasts with the lighter *piano nobile* above. The ground floor contains three bedrooms, bathroom and study, where a long bookcase is set against a frosted glass wall. Light diffuses through the wall, so that the books appear to hover in space. The upper floor, which contains the living and dining spaces, is conceived as a light-filled eyrie floating above the more solid floor below. The rooms on this floor are wrapped in a skin of alternating transparent and translucent glass panels which filter views and engender a sense of privacy. Solid panels of *iroko*, a tropical hardwood, are designed to the same proportions and can be opened to allow ventilation.

A main staircase encased in translucent polycarbonate sheeting on the outside of the building links the two floors and reads as a diaphanous tube. Just visible through the translucent cladding, a steel frame provides the necessary structural support. The staircase tube is terminated at ground level by a vivid blue door, forming the sole element of colour and drawing attention to the point of entry. Cantilevered from the staircase structure, the doorstep is a thin textured sheet of industrial steel. The tube projects around the door and is sliced off at an angle to form a small porch. Strips of *iroko* run across the garden to the street, directing visitors to the entrance.

The overall effect is engagingly undomestic. Industrial materials mix with a tautly refined approach that in its sophisticated play of transparency and translucence recalls the rice paper screens (*shoji*) of traditional Japanese houses. Japanese architecture exerted a profound influence on early European Modernists, who admired the simplicity and spatial egalitarianism of traditional Japanese structures, and Moussafir's elementally simple and light suburban house draws on and extends this relationship.

left The raw blue of the vividly coloured door forms the focus of the enigmatic, planar composition, drawing attention to the point of entry. The door terminates a staircase tube attached to the exterior of the house.

Upper level floor plan

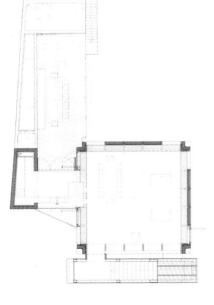

above Inside the staircase, which is enclosed by sheets of translucent polycarbonate cladding, industrial materials are ingeniously used on a domestic scale with assurance and refinement.

35

CHRISTOPHE LAB
PRIVATE RESIDENCE, PARIS, 2000

Paris is, historically, a city of apartment dwellers. Individual houses are relative rarities, but occasionally opportunities arise to create a different sort of dwelling, either by designing a new building or by adapting an existing structure. Christophe Lab was asked to design a new house for a young client who works in the film industry. The brief required two bedrooms and since the client works partly at home, he also needed a study.

The site lies in the seventeenth *arrondissement*. Hemmed in by buildings on either side, the two-storey house steps up the site, with the upper floor projecting over the lower level. From the street, the house presents an enigmatic face. Entry is by means of a gleaming aluminium door that extends the width of the site. The door pivots up, like a giant mouth, giving access to a garage, with the house beyond. In its taut, burnished sleekness, the door has more in common with aeronautics than architecture.

Given his client's occupation, Lab has elaborated on filmic references, exploring the idea of the house as a kind of *camera obscura* in which light travels from one end to the other. The problem of bringing light into the centre of a long, narrow plan has been solved by means of a cylindrical shaft, painted a soft yellow, that penetrates the middle of the house. On the ground floor, the dining area is placed directly underneath, so that diners appear as actors on an illuminated stage. To one side is the kitchen and stairwell, on the other, the living room flows into a small garden through a full-height glass wall. Smoothly sliding doors in slim metal frames dematerialize the boundary between inside and out.

Like the ground floor, the first floor revolves around the cylindrical lightwell. It is reminiscent of a viewfinder, underscoring the cinematic metaphor Lab has used throughout. The two bedrooms are placed at each end of the house, with an open-plan study in the middle. At the north end, the bedroom window is pulled back to form a receding bay behind a balcony and on the south side, the bay is extended.

left *The motorized garage door lifts up to reveal the entry to the house. This unusual device lends an appropriate level of surprise and drama to what is otherwise a polite Parisian façade.*

right *The large glazed doors to the garden appear to be pinned in place by the mass of the upper storey looming above. The effect is intensified by the angular geometry, and the uncanny resemblance of the upper storey to a projection room overlooking a cinema interior.*

Longitudinal section through the house

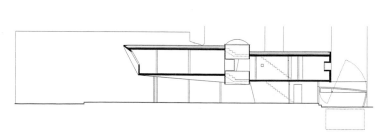

KEN SHUTTLEWORTH
CRESCENT HOUSE, WILTSHIRE, 1997

Set on a site in rural Wiltshire, the house that Ken Shuttleworth designed for himself and his family is a finely judged synthesis of mass and lightness, opacity and transparency. The expansive, concave glass wall of Crescent House affords brief glimpses of brightly lit living spaces within. But visitors must first approach from the rear, where a solid curved white wall dominates, glowing eerily in the crepuscular light.

Gradually the design is revealed. The plan is based on two interconnected crescents – one transparent glass, the other white – with entrances at the end of a sliver-like intermediate space, which doubles as a gallery for displaying the children's art. The glass crescent is oriented south–east towards the garden. The other is slightly different in its alignment, so that the tall gallery between the two tapers in width from south to east. The main entrance is a 3m (10ft) wide door under a concrete wall that doubles as a lintel. Made of aluminium, the massive door pivots open with great ceremony to admit visitors.

In the glass part of the house are the functions associated with communal family life, all elegantly contained within a continuous curved space which opens at each end. Enclosed by a seamless 72m (79ft) long, concave façade of flat glass panels, this garden room wraps around a grassy lawn. Roughly in the middle is a break in the outer wall of the living area, where the space opens across the clerestory-lit gallery to a huge fireplace. This warms the living and dining areas and marks the centre of the house.

The other crescent is, in some ways, just as remarkable as the delicately sheer glass wall. The bedroom crescent has no windows; instead daylight is introduced through a continuous skylight on the outer rim of the curve and the beds are aligned so that their occupants can lie looking up at the moon and stars or listening to the rain and the wind on the glass. These private chambers form a complete contrast to the flowing, curved space of the living area and resemble cells within a medieval castle's walls. The bedroom crescent supplies protection as well as privacy, while the concave crescent of clear glass warms the internal spaces, maximizes daylight and enhances contact with nature. The extreme transparency of the garden façade becomes particularly apparent when the interior is illuminated at night, revealing the white volume of the main living space. Inspired by romantic notions of a precious primordial landscape, the house also embraces the reality of modern rural life.

right *The pivoting entry door terminates the journey from exterior to interior via the sweeping concrete arms of the two crescents that dominate the design concept for the house.*

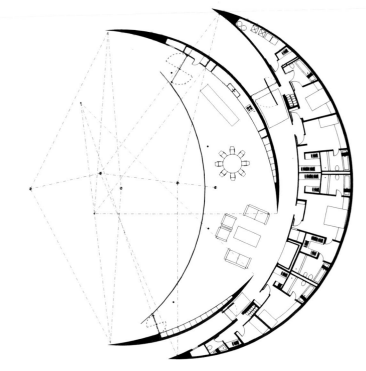

Ground floor plan

above left *At night, the glazed wall of the living room dominates the elegant composition, while the entry presents a glowing eeriness to the night.*

above right *Bathed in full sunlight, the living spaces benefit from natural light all day as the sun travels from east to west, from the living room towards the kitchen.*

left *From the inside, the door terminates the curving top-lit gallery space of the entry hall, where the white walls provide a neutral backdrop for children's colourful artwork.*

HERBERT LEWIS KRUSE BLUNCK
STICKS INC. HEADQUARTERS AND STUDIO, DES MOINES, 1999

Sticks is an artists' studio specializing in contemporary art objects made from fallen timber. The setting – a mature oak grove on the western edge of Des Moines in Iowa – was crucial both to the economics and to the design of the steel-and-concrete building. Aiming to save as many trees as possible, the architects designed the steel-framed structure on a concrete slab that could be tailored to the site, with a curve on the north side to admit light for studios. The north-west corner has a three-sided glazed space used as a communal dining and meeting area, and the west façade is pulled back from the columns and roof beams, revealing a row of inverted L-shapes which form a skeletal colonnade. Throughout, floors are left exposed with the concrete unfinished. Steel roof beams, columns and studs along with ceiling insulation are likewise left exposed. This reliance on natural materials is a hallmark of HLKB's approach and it also reflects Sticks' simple, folk-art roots.

Between each structural bay is a pair of massive mahogany double doors, each inscribed with the wood-burned and painted designs characteristic of Sticks-designed furniture. The monumental doors are 4.1m (13ft 6in) high and 1.2m (4ft) wide and, when open, extend the studio into the site. The pair of doors at the north end of the colonnade form the building's public entrance. With the meeting and design spaces as flanking arms, the showroom-cum-gallery is the culmination of the entry sequence, as well as the culmination of the design and embellishment processes. The project, which optimizes the production process while promoting an inspirational communal working environment, is the fruit of artists and architects determined to create a distinctive architectural language within the context of a prosaic building type.

left *Inside the studio building, bays between the regular structural grid are left open to facilitate movement through the interior. These double-height openings frame the massive timber doors along the façade.*

right *With their intricately decorated surfaces, the huge doors contrast strikingly with the formal composition and the industrial detailing of the rest of the building.*

Exterior elevation

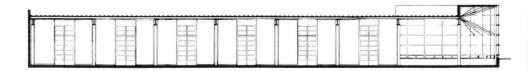

USHIDA FINDLAY
SOFT & HAIRY HOUSE, IBARAKI, 1996

Underscored by an increasing formal and material ingenuity, Ushida Findlay's developing lexicon of houses demonstrates that architecture can reconcile the human need to be in touch with nature. The origins of their style may lie in the unique combination of two passionate streams of consciousness – Celtic and Japanese, representing the ethnicity of the two partners – that appropriates the world through winding and coiling, inscriptions and myths. Yet theirs is an architecture also engaged with the deeper understanding of space, which can be seen throughout their work in the mathematical representation of organic forms such as shells, nests and spiralling growth patterns.

The evocatively named Soft and Hairy House was designed for a young couple, both architectural journalists, and their small child. More than a flight of fantasy, it was an attempt to liberate both client and architect from the socially cohesive, orthodox view of family housing in Japan. Located in Ibaraki, a featureless suburb of Tokyo, the house is an abstract manifestation of the couple lying together with their child cradled in between them. In practical terms, the living, sleeping and cooking spaces are wrapped around a central courtyard, so the house presents a hermetic face to the outside world. The sinuous contours of the plan embody a landscape of the familiar and unfamiliar. A striking and sensuous tactility pervades the interior: walls are swathed in canvas drapes, a door is covered in fake fur and luxuriantly hairy foliage overhangs from the roof.

Within this extraordinary setting is a bathroom that resembles a kind of contemporary igloo. Protruding through a glass wall into the house's internal courtyard, the bathroom pod evokes primeval memories of caves and burrows. Painted a deep midnight blue, the external surface is studded with translucent glass discs that glow softly like stars. Inside, the pod is lined with circular mosaic tiles. A large porthole faces onto the courtyard so that the family can enjoy the view while luxuriating in the bath. Instead of being shut away, the bathroom becomes the visual and geometric fulcrum of the house. The outer face of the bathroom door is wrapped in fake fur, with its overtones of hedonism and luxury. By contrast, the inner face is clinically white, suggesting health and hygiene.

Blue stones inscribed with the words "dream", "dread", and "desire" are positioned around the house, adding to the surreal character of the interior. Designed to stimulate the senses, Ushida Findlay's synthesis of playfulness and voluptuousness generates an example of truly remarkable architecture.

right *The fur-clad bathroom door opens into a glowing, white-tiled pod, hovering ambiguously between the house and the courtyard.*

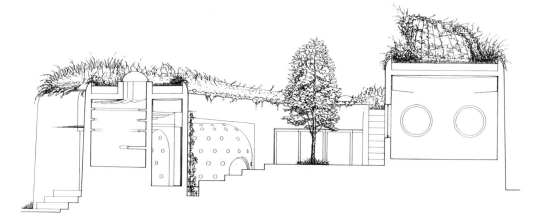

Exterior elevation

above left *From within, the bathroom inspires recollections of science-fiction fantasy. From this perspective, the door becomes a hatch in the moulded surfaces of the walls.*

above *The fur door, surrounded by the soft draping folds of fabric give no clue as to the real character of the pod's interior.*

right *From above, the blue bathroom pod is seen poking out into the courtyard. The main entrance to the house is tucked into a shallow alcove on the street façade, and topped with "soft and hairy" landscaping.*

FRANCIS SOLER
RUE EMILE DURKHEIM APARTMENTS, PARIS, 1998

left *The multi layering of vertical surfaces in the façade results in a shimmering refraction of light and shade, so it is difficult to distinguish what is solid and what is not. The unsettling perspectival distortion is enhanced by the multi-coloured patterned glass.*

right *The straightforward orthogonal structure is given a twist of humour and unexpected whimsy by the exuberant decorative treatment.*

Flanking the monumental Bibliothèque Nationale de France, Francis Soler's apartment block provides a colourful foil for Dominique Perrault's library towers. Built as part of the new residential district on former railway land to the east and west of the library, Soler's block contains subsidized rental housing for middle-income tenants in the form of ninety-three apartments, together with a crèche and underground car-parking.

Designed to cut costs, the block has the virtue of constructional simplicity. Floor slabs, perimeter columns and central spine (where the communal stairs and lifts are located) were cast *in situ* before the dry-mounted partitions and party walls were erected.

Soler's long-standing personal preoccupation with fully glazed façades led him to design the external walls of the flats in the form of a parallel layer of floor-to-ceiling sliding doors separated by a ventilated air gap. Equipped with retractable privacy screens in the air gap, as well as manually operated external sun blinds and narrow, projecting balconies, the sliding doors provide the requisite level of thermal insulation for public housing as well as insulation from noise. But it is the doors' decorative treatment that is the most striking. Soler has put repetitive figurative images resembling outsize translucent colour transfers on the glass of the outer layer of sliding doors. Each storey has its own set of motifs, which are based on details from Giulio Romano's "Feast of the Gods" fresco at the Palazzo del Te in Mantua, reassembled in the manner of Roman Cieslewicz – a dual provenance intended to signal a modern reinterpretation of the past.

The wisdom of so adorning the glass of subsidized rental housing has been questioned – rightly, for living at close quarters with such large omnipresent figurative images could prove oppressive. But, as Soler maintains, his building is designed to allow for future conversion so the decorated glass might be replaced – with clear, differently patterned or opaque glass, or even with solid panels. In any case, by rejecting the usual array of overstated gestures encouraged by the French competition system, Soler contrives to provide an antidote to the bland monumentality of Perrault's Bibliothèque.

Exterior elevation

49

WILLIAMS & TSIEN
MANHATTAN RESIDENCE, NEW YORK, 1997

Compressed into the narrow footprint of two demolished brownstone buildings in a New York City block, this townhouse suggests that it is still possible to build a comfortable, single family dwelling within the super-dense urban fabric of Manhattan. Located on a cross street on the Upper East Side, the architects had to reconcile the disparate scale of the new house's immediate surroundings, which include a thirty-storey tower and neighbouring fifteen-storey brownstones. Williams & Tsien achieved this by putting a great panel of hammered grey Indiana limestone in the middle of the street elevation and allowing the glazing to flow around it. The wall provides a sense of protection and privacy, while at the same time connecting the house with the surrounding fabric through material and scale. The glass, which has a greenish tinge and is held in dark-grey metal glazing bars, ranges from transparent at the upper floor level to translucent at lower levels, thus maintaining privacy while also admitting softly filtered light through to the interior. The rear south wall, which faces the garden, is almost entirely transparent, opening up the house to the sun.

Within the tautly planar stone and glass composition of the street façade, the main entrance is asymmetrically placed at the left-hand corner of the house. Protected by a porch lined with stone, the recessed doorway echoes the theme of geometric planes of glazing set in metal frames. The door opens out into an entrance hall which has an imposing staircase that connects the six storeys of the house. A large skylight brings daylight down through the staircase void, flooding the interior with light. The internal organization is broadly that of an urban terraced house, albeit on a very grand scale. The basement contains a swimming pool, and there is a family kitchen and dining area on the ground floor. The *piano nobile* first floor contains the main setpiece living space, with a study and library. Bedrooms, guest rooms and staff quarters occupy the upper levels. Throughout, spaces and materials are handled with propriety. Floors are made of stone and cherrywood and cherry is also used for the cabinetwork and balustrade rails. Walls and ceilings are simple white skimmed plasterboard, providing a neutral foil for the client's collection of contemporary art.

While this house was evidently designed for a wealthy client, it is also a good neighbour, contributing to the vitality and fabric of the urban realm. Moreover, it affirms the city as a civilized setting for family life, thereby providing an example to those who flee the metropolis each evening for dormitory communities in the suburbs.

right *From the street, the house maintains a polite proportional relationship with its historical neighbours, while at the same time exhibiting a forthright modernity that reflects the contemporary nature of the interior. The entry door, tucked into the right-hand corner, maintains the scale of the street.*

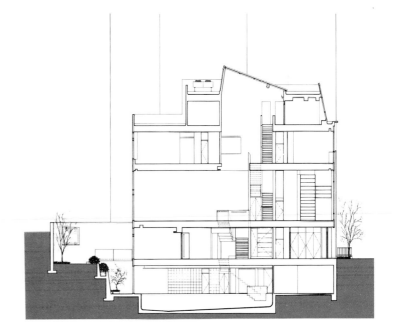

left *The door itself is as minutely considered in its composition as the entire façade. Composed of flat planes cut by vertical and horizontal bars, the whole effect, including the placement of the letter box, resembles an abstract painting.*

above *The entry lobby, a functional yet elegant space, is characterized by the cherrywood used for the joinery and the glazing framework.*

Longitudinal section

Perspective sketch

above The massive limestone bench appears to be effortlessly bisected by the frameless glazing that separates the kitchen and the garden.

JOHN PAWSON
PAWSON HOUSE, LONDON, 1999

John Pawson's latest house for his family lies in a leafy enclave of West London. For Pawson, architecture is a direct reflection of an attitude to life, of taking pleasure in simplicity and restraint and his home eloquently expresses these values. Dating from the mid-nineteenth century, Pawson's house belongs to a tradition of London domestic architecture that used classical embellishments in the pursuit of urban dignity. Despite its modest proportions, it was built with considerable social and architectural ambition, and would originally have been quite a grand family home. From the outside, there is little sense of the transformation within. As with his previous house, Pawson has restored the shell, but completely gutted the interior, tempering the verticality of the original standard plan by introducing a strong horizontal emphasis. On the lower floors, rooms run from front to back and flow into terraces, the linearity of the spaces reinforced by a long stone bench or kitchen counter stretching the length of the house and beyond into the garden courtyard.

The key to the reorganization is a single-flight staircase climbing up from ground floor level that opens up the plan, creating a 4m (13ft) wide unencumbered band of space. As in previous schemes, Pawson has rendered the stairway as an almost mystical place, unadorned and illuminated by a single shaft of light. At the rear of the house the ground-floor kitchen has been projected forwards into the garden, with a terrace above it. The division between interior and exterior is minimized and full-height glass sliding doors held in slim metal frames add to the sense of seamlessness and dematerialization. An immense limestone-clad bench runs the length of one wall, through the glass into the garden, and with daylight filtering through the white-veiled windows and the glass walls at the back, generates a soft, honeyed luminescence. Transformed beyond recognition, the Victorian shoebox is now a place of spatial fluidity, light and tranquillity.

above *From the courtyard, the glass doors slide back to reveal the full length of the bench (nearly 20m / 65ft) which runs continuously from the front façade to the end of the garden.*

55

PUBLIC FAÇADES

Since medieval times, when elaborately carved doorways disseminated the word of God to an illiterate populace, and marked the transition between the sacred and the profane, the door has acted as a means of articulating and expressing the wider aims of architecture. Porticos and porches give added importance to doorways, emphasizing their civil, religious or social significance. Aspects such as the scale of the entrance, the sequence of entry and choice of materials can all be orchestrated to evoke awe, anticipation, intimidation, or excitement, depending on the function of a particular building. From the monumental portico of the remodelled Reichstag in Berlin – a daunting expression of democracy and national identity – to Oscar Niemeyer's pink ramp spiralling up to an art museum spaceship, the doorway has many public faces.

right *Depending on the function of a building and the nature of its relationship with the public, the scale of the entrance, the sequence of entry, and choice of materials can all be calculated to evoke a sense of awe, anticipation, intimidation or excitement. Front entrance and solar panels at The Solar Office, Duxford International Business Park, UK, by Studio E. Architects.*

right *The intensity of the Mediterranean light creates a dramatic triangular shadow on the courtyard floor, while the overhanging roof shades the work spaces.*

ALBERTO CAMPO BAEZA
BALEARIC TECHNOLOGY CENTRE, MALLORCA, 1998

Designed by Madrid-based architect Alberto Campo Baeza, the Balearic Technological and European Business Innovation Centre houses a combination of development agencies and is seen as a showcase and symbol of confidence in the future. The building lies on the fringe of Inca on the island of Mallorca, surrounded by a sprawl of factories and showrooms. Campo Baeza's response is to enclose the triangular site with high walls. Planar and sculptural, with a colour spectrum from white to off-white, the building has little of the stiffness or pedantry often found in minimalist art and architecture. Practically the entire triangular site is taken up by a blind box made of *piedra marés*, a local sandstone. Evoking Islamic architecture, its hermetic limits give no hint of the secret garden it shelters within.

A fold in the wall near one of the corners of the triangle invites visitors to enter. Pedestrian access is up a gentle ramp or adjacent steps running along a short façade just before it turns a forty-five degree corner back along the south-facing hypotenuse. The slight shift in the alignment of this entrance façade creates a sense of place or terrace before the visitor moves inwards. A contiguous lid of flat roof floats overhead, so that entry is experienced not as a traditional punched opening, but as a gap formed by the primary building components.

Axonometric

above *Stepping up to a stone platform from the street, the courtyard, with its peaceful grove of trees is revealed through an opening in the otherwise impenetrable outer wall.*

The courtyard is enclosed by three wings of office space, separated from the perimeter by a linear interstitial terrace. Campo Baeza has placed rooms not in need of constant daylight, such as classrooms, a garage and an auditorium, in a semi-basement which is reached internally via open stairwells, one towards each apex of the plan, or by a glazed hydraulic elevator, which adds to the compositional interest of the entrance area. Frameless glazing and uninterrupted travertine flooring merges the offices with the courtyard garden, with its grid of orange trees. The homogeneity of the courtyard slab is broken only by a sunken meeting room that appears amid the trees, like an open-air *agora*. Inside the office wings, transverse partitions of beechwood are conceived as pieces of furniture and the roof above cantilevers out to keep the work areas in deep, cool shade. The formal and material austerity of Campo Baeza's approach is tempered by a tactility and Mediterranean sensuousness.

ARQUITECTONICA
DIJON AUDITORIUM, DIJON, 1998

Floor plan

Designed by the Miami-based architectural practice Arquitectonica, Dijon's new auditorium in the Clemenceau-Boudronnée district was intended to act as a catalyst for the regeneration of a bleak exposition site, which presently houses a 1950s convention centre and exhibition halls. The triangular plot of land designated for the auditorium is separated from the exposition site by a busy four-lane boulevard. Arquitectonica's design spans the two plots with a glass-enclosed bridge, dramatically pierced by an elliptical lightwell. Known for punching large apertures in building façades, here the architects carved a hole in the bridge floor to allow daylight to reach the street below. Visitors enter from ground level by climbing a large spiral stair or by taking an escalator to the lobby bridge. The elevated lobby opens up into a foyer with the main hall beyond.

The building's sinuous profile and boldly juxtaposed geometric shapes are a familiar part of Arquitectonica's vocabulary. The design reinforces the site's constraints by superimposing two angular, wedge-like shapes, which are splayed in opposing directions and are reminiscent of a grand piano. Punctured by oblong windows at random heights, the stone façade reinforces the musical metaphor by suggesting piano keys.

The great volume of the main hall forms the focus of the building. Through a lively combination of materials,

colours and textures, the hall echoes the shapes and geometrical juxtapositions of the overall architecture. Painterly graphic details are achieved through the use of wood, stone and marble. This strong, decorative approach extends to the doors of the main hall. Paired sets of double doors are enlivened through curved wedges of light and dark wood veneer, which form a sensuous wave-like pattern across the doors. Oval portholes and custom-designed door handles complete the elegant, Art Deco-inspired composition.

The 1,600 seat hall can accommodate ensembles ranging from a 120-member symphony orchestra to a quartet and can be used for seminars and lectures as well as musical performances. Two centuries after the opening of Dijon's Grand Théâtre opera house, the city now has another grand performance space.

above *The long curved street façade is topped with a formally expressed elevated lobby, with punched-out holes opening up the building to the city.*

right *The decorative surface treatment is carried through into the interior where the auditorium doors are clad strikingly in contrasting timber veneers and punched with elliptical windows.*

FRANK GEHRY
GUGGENHEIM MUSEUM, BILBAO, 1998

left *From a plaza where pedestrians approach from the city side of the building, an enormous staircase descends toward the main entrance. While the doors are human in scale, the entry itself is dwarfed by the twisting fluid forms of the building above.*

below *Secondary entrances allow access to and from various parts of the building, offering opportunities to appreciate the building and the city from different perspectives.*

The Guggenheim Foundation has an acute awareness of the power of a building to define an institution. The choice of Frank Gehry to design a new outpost in Bilbao in northern Spain signalled an ambition to match (if not supersede) the radical and original qualities that characterized Frank Lloyd Wright's gleaming Expressionist vortex on Fifth Avenue in New York. The prominence and exposure of the riverside site is curiously well-suited to Gehry's architecture, which generally works best on a *tabula rasa*. The building languidly scrolls and coils its way along the riverside, its boggling conflation of titanium-clad forms shimmering serenely like a pile of improbably huge fish or a fractured tinfoil flower.

From the plaza on the south side visitors begin the carefully choreographed sequence of entry, descending a ceremonial flight of limestone steps pausing, perhaps, to inquisitively fondle the titanium cladding that comes just within reach. The steps gradually narrow, like a canyon, propelling them through a set of doors into a bulging, porch-like protuberance that marks the main entrance. To the right inside the entrance hall is a kind of man-made fissure from which visitors enter the atrium, the spectacular fulcrum of Gehry's whirling volumes. The soaring, 50m (54½ft) high space (one and a half times the height of the rotunda in the New York Guggenheim) stimulates fanciful free association – it evokes Marilyn Monroe's wind-assisted skirts or the moulded sinews of a Willem de Kooning drawing. Light is diffused through slashes of glazing in the inclined walls, casting perpetually changing shadows through the lustrous, luminous, cathedral-like space. On its north side, stone and titanium are peeled away to reveal a soothing water garden.

Despite its complexity, the plan is really quite simple. Nineteen galleries of varying size and configuration are arranged in three storeys around the dramatic, pivotal atrium, so that progress around the building is logical and circuitous, by means of walkways, stairs and glazed lifts. The vast, sculptural spaces offer provocative opportunities for both artists and curators. Through its phenomenal vigour and material presence, Gehry's Guggenheim squares up to both its context and the ambitious mandate of its client, while sustaining a logic of its own.

Design sketch

above *A sweeping bridge, running from one side of the building to the other, defines the edge between the bustling river and the stillness of a reflecting pool.*

right *Inside the entry foyer, the logic-defying geometry of the predominantly glazed roof, provides a fragmented window from which to glimpse framed vignettes of the building.*

YOSHIO TANIGUCHI
HIGASHIYAMA KAII GALLERY, NAGANO, 1990

This art museum, designed by Yoshio Taniguchi, one of Japan's leading architects, is in a corner of Shiroyama Park in the centre of Nagano City. It was built to house a collection of paintings by landscape artist Kaii Higashiyama, who was strongly influenced by the surrounding Japanese landscape. The new building sits in the south-east part of the site, with the remaining portion landscaped and transformed into a formal garden with a reflection pool that is laid with a surface of pale blue-grey stones, expressing an abstraction of nature. The garden is enclosed by a low horizontal wall to screen and frame views of the landscape in the ancient Japanese gardening tradition of *shakkei*, meaning "borrowed landscape".

The geometrically precise form of the museum emphasizes the distinction between it and the existing buildings. Crisp planes of extruded aluminium cladding are reflected in the surrounding pool. The delicate vertical lines of the cladding and the way the building harmonizes with the transparency of the water help to dematerialize it.

The main entrance is an important framing device. An L-shaped staircase leads from the park to a small entrance terrace where double doors of slatted cedar are sheltered by an aluminium-clad porch supported on cylindrical columns. The doorway frames and isolates a view through the entrance hall to the pool courtyard and the landscape beyond. Frozen as if in a painting or photograph, the vista is designed to entice visitors inside; it also suggests something of the building's function.

Exhibition rooms, designed in a deliberately simple manner, with white walls, soft lighting and warm maple floors, are intended as neutral backdrops for the contemplation of Japanese landscape art. Once they have completed their tour, visitors return to the ground floor by a dramatic double-height lightwell. At the end of the route is a meditative space which provides another carefully framed view of nature in the surrounding pool and garden. This real landscape forms a serene conclusion to the visit.

left *From the external façade of the gallery, the entry doors frame a view of the tranquil internal courtyard.*

above *The smooth high walls of the galleries, broken only by a roofed porch, provide a contained backdrop to the water garden at the literal and metaphorical centre of the design.*

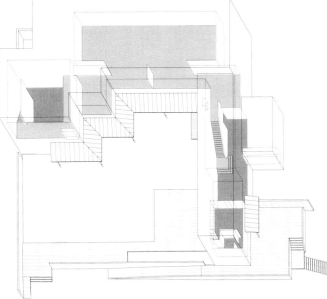

Axonometric

D' AUDIENCE N° 5

JEAN NOUVEL
LAW COURTS, NANTES, 2000

Jean Nouvel's newly completed law courts in Nantes in western France is the product of a wide-ranging review of the French justice system. A tangible result of this reorganization has been an ambitious programme to construct a new generation of regional court buildings in over twenty *départments*. The French Ministry of Justice has emerged an enlightened client, using architectural competitions to elicit a succession of bold contemporary designs.

Nouvel's law courts add to the country's growing stock of gestural essays by eminent architects. The building stands on an island at the point where the Loire divides in two, looking across the river to the centre of Nantes. Around the site arc the decaying hulks of factories and warehouses – the detritus of a thriving industrial and maritime past. Contained in an austere black box of steel and glass, the law courts form the spearhead of long-awaited regeneration. As an exercise in mathematical abstraction, the building is extreme, a temple consecrated to the pure and rather daunting ideals of justice.

On the north side, facing the town, a portico with slender steel columns rises three storeys high to support a projecting floor of offices above. The imposing portico heralds an immense lobby that runs across the entire width of the building. Behind this space are a trio of self-contained boxes housing the main courtrooms. Inside, the rationality of the architecture is subverted in signature Nouvel fashion with a darkly surreal imagination. The glazed lobby rises up to a gridded ceiling, its huge scale rendering visitors Lilliputian by comparison. At the rear of the lobby is a black metal screen, perhaps uncomfortably reminiscent of a prison cage. Underfoot, the mirror-like sheen of the black floor creates a tantalizing play of shifting light and reflections. The tall walls of the courtroom boxes have surfaces like chiselled cliff faces, composed of projecting and indented black wooden blocks. The surfaces of the doors to each courtroom have a similar treatment, so that when closed, they seem to disappear into the wall. Inside, the courtrooms are lined with wood, stained and painted a deep blood red. Oblique shafts of light dramatically illuminate each space. To move from the inky gloom of the lobby to the crimson wombs of the courts is to experience a thrillingly unexpected transition.

left *The layering of black grids and the reflective, polished floor conspire almost to conceal the entrances to the courts, which are in the textured, slightly recessed panels in the wall.*

In an age cushioned by euphemism, Nouvel's brooding law courts are slightly shocking and undeniably theatrical. Rejecting the present vogue for disguising courthouses as arts centres, Nouvel's building is a merciless yet coolly calculated expression of the power of justice.

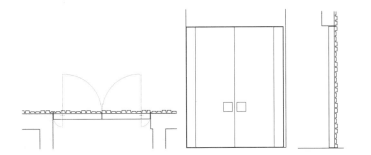

Plan and elevation of courtroom doorway

above left *The three-storey high portico marches along the riverfront, where the strip of offices above can just be seen.*

right *The entry portico, with its gridded surfaces and regular columns, provides a bold transition from the public to the judicial realms.*

above right *In contrast to the public spaces, the courtrooms are treated with warm timber panelling, which are lit by skylights; the only source of natural light in the chamber. Again, the courtroom doors almost disappear into the timber grid of the rear wall.*

VON GERKAN MARG & PARTNERS
UNDERGROUND STATION, BIELEFELD, 1991

The work of Von Gerkan Marg & Partners typifies the best new public architecture in Europe. Founded in the mid-1970s by Meinhard von Gerkan and Volkwin Marg, the practice has become a considerable force in contemporary German (and hence European) architecture, with buildings in most major German cities. With its roots in rational Modernism and the engineering tradition, it embraces a great range of projects and architectural responses. Yet this is not simply a matter of canny stylistic variation. Von Gerkan Marg's breadth of approach reflects a belief that the diversity of design expresses the wider diversity of life.

The remodelling of the main railway station in the northern German town of Bielefeld has both high drama and cool logic. Its principal feature is the skilful use of light. A huge wedge of glass brings daylight down into the station's subterranean platforms. This glazed, tented roof marks the entrance to the station and also forms a civic landmark. Two escalators enclose a central stair and the gentle pitch of the roof follows the shallow angle of the escalator descent. The canopy is composed of a series of triangular planes. In plan, the roof is triangular and both side elevations describe acute-angled triangles. The entrance portal is also triangular. Panes of clear toughened glass are suspended from a series of angular steel trusses and a row of light fittings hang from the roof's central spine. Below ground, a wide concourse leads to the station platforms.

The use of pure geometric form and the transparency of the roof make the station entrance visible from a distance, becoming a symbol of the transition to an underground realm. In mythology, the passage from the earth's surface to the underworld usually has profound symbolic overtones, but this is a more prosaic threshold, used by streams of local commuters (who when they emerge from the station, catch sight of Von Gerkan Marg's project, Bielefeld's City Hall). Nevertheless, the architects manage to infuse it with a sense of theatre, through the orchestration of space and light. Meticulously constructed, with a clear civic presence, the station roof epitomizes Von Gerkan Marg's ability to move effortlessly from bold large-scale gestures to intricate detailing. Their architecture has a totality of approach that is rarely seen in architects whose work is so diverse.

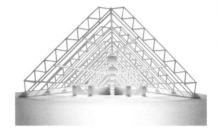

Perspective

right *Sitting low to the ground, the simple clarity of the glass and steel structure appears to be a kind of minimalist intervention in the landscape.*

below *The triangular glass roof lends a certain grandeur historically associated with the grand age of rail travel as passengers descend into the subterranean station.*

Floor plan

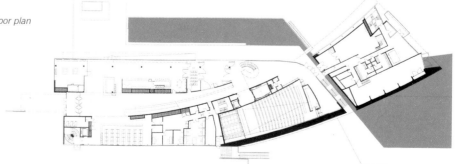

above *A vertical blade in the museum's forecourt acts as a sentinel, outside the entry space.*

STEVEN HOLL
MUSEUM OF CONTEMPORARY ART, HELSINKI, 1998

The outcome of a major international architectural competition, Steven Holl's Museum of Contemporary Art in Helsinki seeks to redefine the image of the museum as elitist treasure house to one of inclusive public meeting place. Factors such as a disparate collection of works, varied events and extended opening hours are all intended to attract the widest possible audience.

The building consists of two contrasting parts: an orthogonal block placed protectively against an adjacent motorway, and a curvilinear extrusion that houses the main suite of gallery spaces. Between these volumes is a canyon-like void containing a long curved ramp that leads up to the circuit of galleries.

Approached across a granite-paved forecourt, the main entrance lies at the south end of the building. A steel-framed glazed canopy extends out from the vertical fissure between the two volumes to draw visitors into the entrance. The main entrance doors are set in a wall partially clad in panels of acid-reddened brass, a material used to mark significant cuts through the building. Beyond the main entrance is a small "decompression lobby" – to enable visitors to shake snow off their boots or stow their umbrellas before entering – from which two glass revolving doors lead into the museum. The outwardly modest demeanour of the entrance façade provides a neutral foil for the interior drama of the warped, elongated void at the heart of the museum.

The permanent collection is housed on the lower galleries, with changing temporary exhibitions on the upper levels. Despite this apparently straightforward allocation of space and function, the underlying order of the building cannot be apprehended from a single vantage point, but unfolds cinematically as visitors move through a landscape of interior spaces. This is an architecture of promenade, but one that always returns to the central void.

Designed to make the most of the elusive quantity and quality of daylight available in this extreme northern latitude, the museum's curved section captures the warm light of a horizontal sun, which is then filtered by carefully placed windows. Much of the daylight in the building – particularly in the galleries and central void – is diffused by translucent glass. This both intensifies the weak Nordic light and imparts to the visitor a sense of quiet abstraction and detachment from the life of the city outside.

above right *The glazed entry space lies sandwiched between a rectangular block and the sweeping curve of the main gallery spaces.*

MARKS BARFIELD
LONDON EYE, LONDON, 2000

Constructed to mark the millennium, and now coming to symbolize London in the way the Eiffel Tower symbolizes Paris, the London Eye is a colossal rotating wheel, 122m (133ft) in diameter, located on a riverside site opposite the Houses of Parliament. Designed by Julia Marks and David Barfield, the wheel is a simple idea executed with great chutzpah, and the public has responded to it with extraordinary enthusiasm.

Unlike a Ferris wheel, where gravity keeps the gondolas horizontal, the curved glass capsules rotate mechanically, remaining outside the structure throughout. This induces a special drama at the top of the half-hour circuit, where you seem to be floating, weightless and unsupported, above the great sprawl of the metropolis. There is no adrenalin rush, rather a sense of dignified dislocation as the wheel revolves slowly and silently.

Fabricated by skilled Italian glassmakers, each capsule resembles a transparent bubble. Motorizing the capsules allowed the passengers to walk around on a level floor and enabled the capsules to be placed on the outer rim of the wheel, enhancing views. Framed with stainless-steel tubes, the wall and roof sections are fully glazed. The glass is a laminate sandwich secured by an adhesive strong enough to resist the pressure of the glass breaking. To achieve the desired aerodynamic shape, the glass had to be double curved, the first time that such a complex form had been executed in laminated glass.

On the landside end of each capsule is a pair of glass sliding doors. Each set of doors is motorized and automatically controlled to slide open while the capsule passes through the boarding platform area. The wheel's rotation is constant, so while the capsules are actually moving, albeit very slowly, passengers must board and disembark. The computers know the position of each capsule in the rotation cycle by interpreting signals from a remote encoder that detects the position of the wheel's central moving hub in relation to the fixed spindles on which the capsules rotate.

Through their vision and ingenuity, Marks and Barfield have given Londoners an unsurpassed new vantage point from which to contemplate their city. As a new civic landmark, the wheel is both obvious and subtle; as a piece of sculpture it appears to be static, yet it is in motion; and as a symbol of the new millennium, its imperceptible movement expresses the very passage of time as well as the cycle of the seasons.

right The doors of the glazed capsule open at the bottom of the circuit to allow passengers to board and disembark as the wheel continues to rotate.

Section and plan of one of the pods

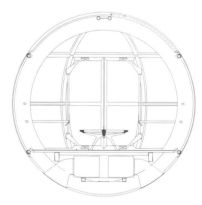

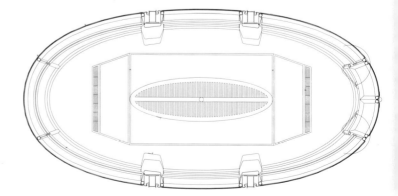

left *Towering over the Houses of Parliament, the Millennium Wheel has, in a surprisingly short time, become a fondly familiar landmark on the River Thames for Londoners as well as visitors to the city.*

above left *Passengers board the pods, suspended from the steel structure of the giant wheel, hanging above the river.*

above right *Once the doors are closed and the capsule rises over the city, spectacular views are revealed of a London previously unseen .*

MECANOO ARCHITEKTEN
DUTCH NATIONAL HERITAGE MUSEUM, ARNHEM, 1999

The Open-Air Museum, which lies in a 18-hectare (44-acre) park within the forest of Arnhem, is structured around a series of eighty buildings from various regions of the Netherlands which embody the historic relationship between the built and natural worlds. It also has impressive collections of costume and jewellery, but until recently had no space to display them. The architects Mecanoo were asked to provide a new set of spaces to house a museum shop, galleries, café and a multimedia theatre.

The landscape, which forms the starting point for the design, is incised by a wall over 140m (460ft) long, that acts both as gateway and spine for the new elements. Composed of brick, it is a rich, rustic mosaic of diverse patterns and textures. Since walls divide, protect and define the Dutch landscape, this elongated structure has a particularly apt historic resonance. Behind the wall, existing and new parts of the museum are slowly revealed. A long lane of oak trees follows the shape of the meadow and determines the position of the entrance gateway in the elongated wall. When the museum is closed, the glazed entrance may be protected by heavy red sliding panels, which look like barn doors, emphasizing the rural connection.

Shaded by a broad-brimmed flat roof, the pavilion is an elegant, timber-framed glass box; it is almost Japanese in its simple, rational austerity. Its ground floor contains a café and terrace, as well as an education centre and information hall. The focus of the lower levels is an egg-shaped multimedia theatre which protrudes above ground like a giant boulder. Clad in a sensuous skin of copper, the centre emerges on the entrance side of the wall, a brooding and tantalizing monolithic presence.

The immediate surroundings of the new museum are carved out of the landscape. Boulders lie along paths as informal seats. At dusk, the complex is lit up, the wall with its myriad textures, the great copper egg and a few solitary trees, creating a strangely entrancing panorama, as curious and compelling as the Dutch landscape itself.

above *The timber and glass entrance foyer, containing a café, information centre and education facility, looks out over the densely landscaped park.*

above *The enormous sliding panels, complete with signage, are slid away from the glazing when the museum is open.*

Exterior elevation

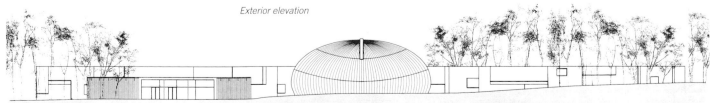

JUHANI PALLASMAA
FINNISH CULTURAL INSTITUTE, PARIS, 1991

left *An urbane composition of steel and translucent glass forms the entrance to the Finnish Institute in Paris. The door is recessed underneath a projecting bay to provide shelter. Crisp detailing combines with a finely honed materiality.*

right *The heavy brass doors provide the first point of contact with the building for visitors.*

The Finnish Institute in Paris is located in the Rue des Ecoles on the Left Bank, near the Sorbonne University. It occupies two floors and a basement in a mid-nineteenth century building originally designed by the influential architect and planner Baron Hausmann. The Institute's varied programme of activities meant that it required facilities for lectures, exhibitions and meetings, together with a library and offices. Coupled with limitations of space, this presented the architects (the Finn Juhani Pallasmaa working with Paris-based Roland Schweitzer and Sami Tabet) with a considerable challenge.

Pallasmaa's remodelling attempts to strike a balance between a modern, specifically Finnish character and the Hausmann building. He divided the frontage into three vertical bays, expressed as steel-framed glass boxes. The lower parts of two of the bays are enclosed by clear glass, to become, in effect, shop windows for the Institute's various events. The upper parts are enclosed in glass that has been sandblasted with horizontal bands, creating privacy for the offices and library, but also allowing glimpses out.

The slightly recessed main entrance is set symmetrically in the central bay. Doors are made of 12mm (½ in) thick solid brass, inset with a grid of tiny glass spyholes. Light percolates through the holes, animating the entrance and softening the austere monumentality of the brass. The perforated door has historical roots as Pallasmaa observes: "It is an important aspect of traditional architecture, light seeping through a heavy door." Door handles are elegant tubular compositions, also in brass. To Pallasmaa, the door handle acts as a kind of touchstone for a building and its emphasis cannot be overstated. "The door handle is your very first physical encounter with a building," he explains. "I think it should be individual, friendly and inviting, not impersonal or standardized."

Inside, furniture and fittings are custom-designed, so that the building reads as a sum of carefully judged and executed parts. As well as the elaboration of detail, the project also emphasizes transparency and the continuity of space. The outcome is an understated yet clearly contemporary spirit, which both expresses a Parisian ambience and signals the Finnishness of the Institute.

Exterior elevation

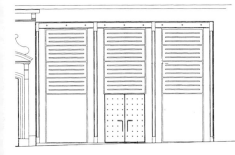

83

BEAUDOUIN PARTNERSHIP
MÉDIATHÈQUE FRANÇOIS MITTERAND, POITIERS, 1996

The history of the French city of Poitiers was distinguished by Roman occupation, of which traces still remain, and a flourishing medieval period. Designed by the husband-and-wife partnership of Laurent and Emmanuelle Beaudouin, the city's *médiathèque,* or media library, is located in the oldest part of Poitiers, straddling a Roman fortress wall which was painstakingly rebuilt and incorporated into the new building.

The architects' challenge was to integrate a large public building within the city's dense, historic core. The *médiathèque* lies next to a large seventeenth-century building which nestles up against some medieval houses and its form takes its cue from this contextual relationship. The notion of adding on elements around a central core volume is derived in part from a notable Romanesque church, Notre-Dame-la-Grande, which stands nearby and has a similarly accretional, irregular form. Implanted deep in the historic urban fabric, the building's basic square geometry is fractured and broken along three of its sides by volumes that hint at some of the internal functions. The fourth side abuts a tightly packed row of medieval houses.

On the east side, the *médiathèque* is pulled back from the existing university building to create an interstitial garden. This forms part of the sequence of entry, but also creates a breathing space between the old and new buildings. A shallow ramp with steps leads up to a tall covered porch created by recessing the entrance from the external wall. The wall is strongly articulated with an outer layer of enamelled glass *brises-soleils* held in a concrete frame. An elegantly detailed set of double doors clad in horizontal bands of blonde wood with triangular steel handles mark the main entrance. Generous proportions and honorific materials add a sense of dignity.

Combining a contemporary spirit with a sensitivity to the past, the Beaudouins' design attempts to achieve some of the fluidity, light and mystery of Le Corbusier's Millowners' building in the Indian city of Ahmedabad.

left *The extended wall of* brises-soleils *protects the glazed façade behind and lends an appropriately monumental scale to this new public building.*

right *The entry, cut into the regular geometry of the screen wall of external skin, terminates a bridge that passes carefully over historical building fragments. The actual doors are dwarfed by the scale of the portico covering them.*

Design sketch

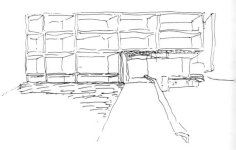

STUDIO GRANDA
MUSEUM OF MODERN ART, REYKJAVIK, 2000

Studio Granda's new Musuem of Modern Art in Reykjavik is an inventive conversion of a harbourside 1930s warehouse. Made of concrete with a distinctive mushroom-headed column structure, the building has a robust dignity and solidity. Its two wings, arranged around a long thin central courtyard, were remodelled by Studio Granda and bisected with an angular spine that follows the line of the original pier for the port of Reykjavik, so the pier's archaeological imprint now underscores the evolution of the new museum. The spine/pier leads from the entrance hall in the south wing through the courtyard, terminating in a tall glazed opening overlooking the harbour. It also links two sets of staircases that lead to the upper floors in each wing. Along the length of the spine, a sumptuous black walnut floor and hot-rolled steel sheets tightly bolted to walls and columns (like a fetishistic metal corset) form a powerful contrast with the mainly white, luminous gallery spaces.

The *parti* is both elegant and economical. Galleries are located in both wings, with the museum café and library housed in the north wing at the end of the spine. Delivery, workshop and storage occupy the ground floor of the north wing, connected to a service entrance on the harbour side. Offices and the museum's architectural archive are located on the second floor of the north wing. Externally, the warehouse has been simply painted in what the architects describe as "Fishery Protection Vessel Grey", with the new museum parts demarcated in white. An angular concrete canopy set in the south flank denotes the main public entrance. Cunningly, the canopy also reflects light into the double-height entrance hall, illuminating its black floor and the steel plate walls that mark the beginning of the spine/pier.

Cutting through the courtyard, the spine/pier forms a large external exhibition space on the east side and double-height white room on the west that can be adapted for various uses. Two hefty steel doors, their scale and materiality recalling the building's industrial origins, open up the spine to the central courtyard. Further sets of tall folding doors reveal the white room beyond. A skylit box illuminates the spine and at night its soft glow washes through the court. This, Studio Granda's latest building, enlivens the rational through sensual use of materials and consolidates the company's growing reputation.

left *Enormous steel doors open up a multi-purpose room to the external exhibition space. Their size, contrasted here with the human scale of the white chairs, recalls the building's industrial past.*

Exterior elevation

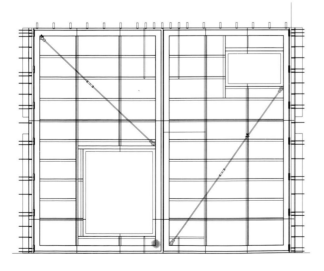

above left and opposite *The striking cantilevered concrete canopy, used to signify the main public entry, boldly heralds the buildings' new use as an art gallery.*

above right *From the central courtyard, the steel doors lend a sense of drama to the central spine of the building, which forms the organizational core of the design.*

OSCAR NIEMEYER
MUSEUM OF CONTEMPORARY ART, RIO DE JANEIRO, 1996

On the east side of Guanabara Bay lies the dormitory suburb of Niterói, the setting for Rio de Janeiro's new Museum of Contemporary Art built to house the paintings and sculptures of one of Brazil's foremost modern art collectors. Formerly spread across the city in various locations, the collection is now unified in a single, remarkable building designed by Oscar Niemeyer.

The new museum occupies a rocky promontory with views east towards Rio and Sugarloaf Mountain. Given the alien quality of Rio's landscape, it seems appropriate that the form of the museum should suggest a flying saucer, effortlessly poised for take-off. Cantilevered out from a central stalk, the saucer-like volume of the building has an unmistakable iconic presence, its seductive sci-fi geometry creating a new landmark for the district.

above *Hovering over the bay, the saucer-like museum has become an architectural icon for Rio de Janeiro.*

left *The long curve of the ramp allows visitors to ascend to the gallery in a ceremonious procession towards the main entry. The drama of the approach is only upstaged by the striking disc of the gallery itself.*

Floor plan

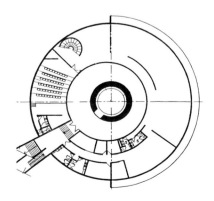

The building's concrete structure consists of three circular floor plates with radii ranging from 18 to 20m (59 to 65½ft). They are supported by a central cylinder 9m (29½ft) in diameter. A serpentine ramp (rendered a coruscating pink) coils up languidly from the surrounding plaza to dock into the flank of the saucer. The elegant interplay of curves is reflected by a circular pool at ground level. Painted a gleaming white, the untreated concrete structure embodies the evocative, monumental quality of Niemeyer's initial sketches. The main entrance, a simple and unceremonious glass door, is set vertically into the angled wall. Apart from this, the building's sole articulation is a broad strip of glazing that wraps around its entire circumference like a visor. Black vertical mullions form a crisp contrast against the white carapace, magnifying the scale and underscoring the building's function as a civic landmark.

The museum saucer has three levels, with staff facilities housed in the lowest floor. The top floor is devoted to installations and temporary displays and the intermediate level houses the permanent collection. Niemeyer neatly overcomes the patent unsuitability of curved walls for the display of art by creating an inner hexagonal-shaped core of space enclosed by flat screen walls. This generates surprising flexibility, although the stunning panoramas of Rio (visible through gaps in the screen walls and in the outer perimeter zone of gallery space) might occasionally upstage the art.

91

WILL BRUDER
SCOTTSDALE CENTER FOR THE ARTS, ARIZONA, 1999

Scottsdale, in the Phoenix conurbation in Arizona, might not yet be renowned as a great regional centre of art, but its citizens are trying in a modest way to implement a programme for new cultural buildings. One successful project is Will Bruder's transformation of a 1970s multiscreen cinema into a Museum of Contemporary Art. The main alterations to the building have been on the east side, where with great thought and sensitivity Bruder has created a front that is gently curved in plan, intended to attract visitors into the building. While the cinema building was executed in drab, dusty stucco, the new façade glitters and shimmers. It also bulges at each end, in homage to the neighbouring Center for the Arts. Unlike many contemporary designers, Bruder has created a museum that encourages the art and its custodians to speak and does not try to overwhelm them with the power of his architecture.

The south end of the new façade is conceived as a huge glass sculpture by the artist James Carpenter. Large sheets of dichroic glass enclose a small sculpture court filling it with ever-changing bands of ravishing green, blue, red and purple light. The rest of the new part, in an attempt to create what Bruder describes as something reminiscent of a handmade quilt, is clad in panels of silver galvanized steel in assorted sizes. Like Carpenter's glass, the metal seems to ripple and iridesce in the clear desert light. Behind the façade, the old building is painted a muted purplish grey.

On entering, you are drawn down the main axis by curves towards the gallery spaces at the rear of the building. These are equipped with differently sized roof lanterns so that the curators can choose to let in shafts and pools of daylight which can be inflected, coloured or simply obscured. But on a sunny day, visitors cannot fail to be drawn to Carpenter's sculpture court. To the left of the main entrance, a crisply detailed steel-and-glass door leads out into the space. Part of the new curved wall extends from inside to wrap around the existing building. A slatted pergola creates a sheltering porch at the sculpture court entrance and Carpenter's enclosing glass wall casts magically coloured shadows through the space, energizing and animating the entire building.

left *The new entry pavilion for the Scottsdale Centre for the Arts is clad in shiny galvanized steel, reflecting the colours and light of the city. The façade curves gently inwards from both ends, encouraging visitors to enter the building.*

right *At one end of the entry pavilion, sheets of dichroic glass are suspended above a small sculpture court, refracting patterns of coloured light onto the ground.*

Floor plan

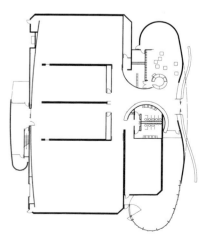

DESIGN ANTENNA
BROADFIELD HOUSE GLASS MUSEUM, KINGSWINFORD, 1995

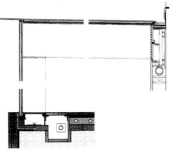

Section

above *The new entry pavilion, constructed entirely of glass for both the cladding and structure, is an entirely appropriate architectural expression for a building that houses one of the most important collections of glass in Europe.*

left *The doors are set within the orthogonal grid of the glazed façade, almost disappearing in the reflective surface.*

Broadfield House Glass Museum at Kingswinford in England's West Midlands is an eloquent expression of the human preoccupation with glass. Ever since the Egyptians fused vitreous surfaces onto stone and clay in around 1500BC, glass has assumed myriad decorative and functional forms, but here it makes the transcendental leap into the realm of structural material. Unusually, this prototypical project exploits the strength of glass in compression; it takes a relatively simple step from using a glass fin as a stiffener and bracing device to using it as a column. The museum's location is apt, for the nearby town of Stourbridge has been associated with glassmaking for four hundred years, particularly during the nineteenth century.

The entrance is housed in a rectangular, flat-roofed pavilion constructed entirely from glass. Exuding formal simplicity and poetic transparency, it belies the ingenuity of its architect, Brent Richards of Design Antenna, and of its engineer Tim Macfarlane of Dewhurst Macfarlane. The glass-panelled skin is supported on a triple-laminated-glass structural frame. Laminated-glass beams at 1.1m (3½ft) centres span 5.7m (18⅔ft) from the rear brick wall to a series of glass columns on the front elevation. The delicate fin-shaped columns are set in metal shoes below ground and are connected to the beams by bonded mortice-and-tenon joints. Both beams and columns were custom-designed and made for the project. The transparent wall plane is made of three layers of glass. An outer, low emissivity layer reduces solar gain and is separated from the two inner panes by a 10mm (⅜in) air gap. The roof uses a similar construction, but the inner layer is printed with a pattern of ceramic bars to diffuse heat gain and glare. In very hot weather an air extract system may be used.

Believed to be one of the largest all-glass buildings ever constructed, the structure is remarkably robust: an earlier domestic conservatory (designed by Rick Mather and engineered by Macfarlane using the same system) even withstood the weight of a somewhat surprised fleeing burglar. The pavilion has an exquisite, mirage-like seamlessness – it seems barely there, yet it marks an intriguing new phase in the evolution of glass.

95

MUSEUM LINER APPENZELL

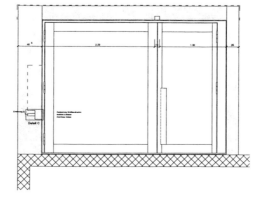

Exterior elevation

GIGON & GUYER
LINER MUSEUM, APPENZELL, 1998

Dedicated to the *oeuvre* of Swiss artists Carl Liner and his son, this modest art museum in the small town of Appenzell is part of an impressive series of gallery and exhibition spaces by the young partnership of Gigon & Guyer. Interpreted as an austere, proto-industrial shed animated by inventive use of materials, the museum's zigzag profile echoes the saddle-roofed houses typical of Appenzell and the sawtooth roofs of industrial and agricultural buildings. The stainless-steel cladding panels allude to the local tradition of buildings sheathed in wood shingles that weather to a silver grey. The sandblasted stainless steel has a chameleon-like character, changing in the mountain climate from shiny to myriad tones.

The south elevation is dominated by a large window to the entrance hall, which forms the building's great cubic snout. The same device is repeated at the north end. The main entrance is a protruding box whose walls seem to fold out from the inside, losing their metal skin along the way to reveal the building's inner layer of concrete. Here the metal cladding is reduced to the roof of the box and the lettering announcing the museum. Doors are floor-to-ceiling glass in stainless-steel surrounds with simple vertical steel tube handles. The vestibule has a south-facing skylight and its big, landscape-scaled window looks out towards the mountains, imbuing the interior with the changing effects of light and climate.

The galleries are intimate and relaxed, yet their architectural language is ambivalent, hovering between a traditional architecture of rooms and an abstract one of planes. Spaces have a minimum of detail; walls and ceiling are white and the grey floor bears the centrifugal pattern left from the finishing process. The collection itself is modest and beloved, for which Gigon & Guyer have designed an appropriately low-tech, low-maintenance and low-budget building that engages in a sophisticated play between outside and inside.

above *Announced by a box attached to the sawtoothed roof of the "shed" of the main gallery, the entry doors themselves are simple, stainless steel framed glass panels.*

above *The architects continue the device of applying boxes and frames to the exterior of the building whenever an opening is required for access, light or ventilation.*

KAZUYO SEJIMA
KUMANO-KODO ART MUSEUM, NAKAHECHI, 1998

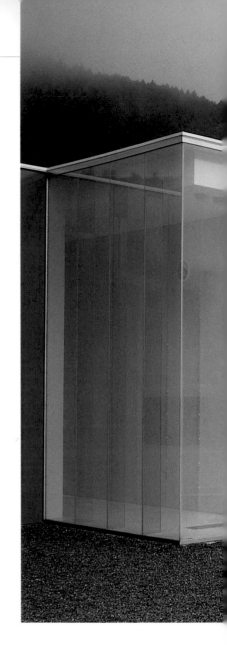

Dedicated to the work of two Japanese painters, the Kumano-Kodo Museum lies outside the town of Nakahechi, south of Osaka. Spreading horizontally against the undulating contours of the terrain, Kazuyo Sejima's diaphanous, glass-skinned building sits lightly on the ground, as if it had just alighted on the site. The resemblance to some form of alien craft is unmistakable (even down to the entrance conceived as a kind of docking port), but this capacity to unnerve is a familiar aspect of Sejima's architecture. As in her previous projects, Sejima's delicately contrived formal and material minimalism draws on Japanese traditions of *kinari*, meaning unadorned beauty.

While the museum's principal function is to house the work of two local artists, it is also a community centre for the town. The main body of the building is an environmentally controlled core of exhibition galleries, surrounded by a buffer zone of public space. From this parent body, two volumes project into the landscape, like the tails of a comet. One houses offices, a library and a lobby; the other gallery access and storage space. Vertical sheets of full-height translucent glass form the building's ethereal outer membrane.

The main entrance is on the east side, where double doors of milkily translucent glass are sheltered by a simple steel porch that curves slightly on plan. The skinny porch marks the end of a narrow, meandering path connecting the building with the main road. This serpentine approach weaves through an expanse of grey gravel and spindly saplings that surrounds the museum like a Zen garden, emphasizing its other-worldly quality.

The communal space enclosing the inner gallery core is furnished with tables and vividly coloured stools like abstract flowers, where visitors can sit and contemplate the view. Throughout, the exquisitely orchestrated tension in the building is a constant source of delight. The crystalline outer walls form a lightweight counterpoint to the more solid core and visitors experience a sequence of receding and advancing planes, which act as an abstract representation of the local topography. Responding to the beauty of the setting and the needs of the local community, Sejima's building is imbued with a powerful yet sensual architectural identity.

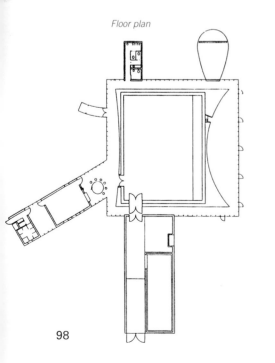

Floor plan

above   A slim metal porch curves out to meet a sinuous approach path through the austere gravel landscape. Enclosed in a diaphanous glass membrane, the building has a sensuous translucence.

right   Views out are veiled through the glass. A fluid outer layer of public space encloses a core of exhibition galleries.

FOSTER & PARTNERS
REICHSTAG, BERLIN, 1999

For decades after the Second World War, the Reichstag sat isolated and neglected on the edge of the Berlin Wall, a brooding, gloomy hulk far from the glittering shops and comfortable apartments of West Berlin. It was hard to believe that such a ruined and historically charged place could ever again be the focus of real democratic political and national life, which makes Foster & Partners' transformation of the Reichstag into the seat of government and a symbolic focus of a unified Germany all the more remarkable.

Most parliaments originated in theatres and with Foster's project, the theatrical makes an undisguised return. The entrance, through the monumental west portico, is as impressive as that of any theatre, and the public galleries project into the main chamber like opera boxes. Furthermore, the spectacular new dome that crowns the building is pure event architecture. Whether glistening in the sun or glowing at night, whether seen from inside from the spectacular ramp that runs through it, or from the nearby Brandenburg Gate, the dome symbolizes the future with an eloquence that no building in the former German capital of Bonn ever achieved.

To reach the dome, visitors have to process through a formal entry sequence. Public accessibility and procedural openness have guided the design. Both public and politicians enter as equals by the same route, a proper expression of the relationship between electors and the elected in a modern democracy. Foster reopened the original entrance up the grand flight of stairs on the west side so that people entering the building are confronted with a direct view of the seats of the President and Chancellor. They arrive in an awesomely tall, thin antechamber, dramatically lit from above. Immediately in front is a glass wall which defines the entrance lobby; beyond is a further transparent partition that allows views into the chamber itself. The heaviness of the original neo-classical portico is tempered by great planes of toughened clear glass held in slim metal frames that define the new entrance route. Despite the inevitable need for security measures in such a prominent public building, the masterful orchestration of space and light instils the mundane process of queuing with a sense of dignity. Once inside, MPs enter the floor of the chamber, while lifts take the public to the roof terrace or mezzanine levels.

In its new incarnation, the Reichstag wears the scars of its history bravely. What stands out is the subtlety of the relationships between old and new, the powerful yet accessible nature of the chamber and the openness of the building, both visual and metaphorical. It embodies the memory of terrible events, but its rebirth is a profound symbol of hope.

100

right Toughened glass screens held in slim steel frames form the new entrance. These provide security but also minimise the visual and physical impact on the original building fabric.

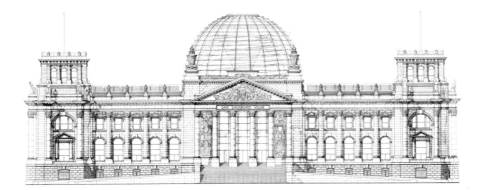

Exterior elevation

above left and right *Part of the revived main elevation, resonating with history and reinvigorated by the light, crisp detailing of the glass curtain beyond the stately stone façade.*

left *The Reichstag's monumental entrance portico dwarfs visitors queuing up for security screening, where both public and politicians enter as equals on the same route.*

103

OUTSIDE IN

Demarcating and dramatizing space, the doorway is often the focus of architectural creativity and imagination. In architecture of almost all types and periods, particular attention has been devoted to the doorway, whether it be a grand entrance or more modest internal door. Like many elements, the door has undergone a fascinating process of evolution and the character of a building can be transformed by the treatment of its openings. Experiments with materials and form continue to produce new and inventive solutions to the apparently simple act of entering a building. In New York, Future Systems borrow technology from boat building to create a seductive, shimmering entrance tunnel to an upmarket clothes store, while in London Philippe Starck gives the revolving door a new twist, by experimenting with scale and colour to devise a theatrical entrance for a chic boutique hotel.

left *Doors and gates demarcate space, establish boundaries and mark thresholds. Experiments with materials and form continue to produce new and inventive solutions, such as here in the Joiner Street entrance to London Bridge Station, by Weston Williams Architects.*

FUTURE SYSTEMS
COMME DES GARÇONS, NEW YORK, 1999

Japanese designer Rei Kawakubo is the driving force behind the Commes de Garçons clothes stores. Her philosophy is more akin to that of sculptor than fashion designer and she is celebrated for her innovative approach to the materials and structure of her clothes. Control of the company image is fundamentally important and extends to the spaces in which the clothes are displayed. Kawakubo has cultivated a fruitful relationship with architect Takao Kawasaki, who has interpreted and given form to her often provocative ideas. Ten years ago notions of movement were the dominant theme, with vividly coloured, fluid interiors, but recently there has been a shift. A family of new shops in New York and Tokyo are intended to express a mood of individuality and experimentation. For these, Kawakubo and Kawasaki have collaborated with the British partnership of Future Systems to create a series of striking, radical designs. New York's Comme des Garçons was the first of the new flagship stores. The chosen location was a dilapidated nineteenth-century industrial building in West Chelsea, an area more usually associated with contemporary art galleries than high fashion boutiques. Rather than refurbish the entire structure, the approach has been to retain the original exterior and insert a new shop behind the anonymous façade of weathered brick and hand-painted signs.

The transition from street to shop is made through a beguiling silver tunnel, the outcome of Future Systems' characteristically inventive approach. Boat-building techniques were used to create an object that has no supporting ribs or spars – the skin and structure are one. The gleaming aluminium gullet is a monocoque, which was cut and assembled to the architects' computer drawings in a boat-builder's workshop in Cornwall. Panels of 6mm (³⁄₁₆ in) thick aluminium are invisibly welded together with seamless joints. Once in place, it was grafted behind the existing brick structure and the aluminium was hand-sanded to produce a seductively lustrous surface that ripples and shimmers in light.

The entrance tunnel is divided by a glazed pivoting door that cuts through the space physically but not visually. A row of glowing red lights is set into the floor. The tunnel disgorges shoppers into a soaring white space, with the clothes inhabiting a surreal landscape of sculptural enclosures made of white enamelled steel. For Kawakubo, the beautifully crafted entrance engenders a sense of exploration and provides a bridge between the gritty street outside and the designer delights within.

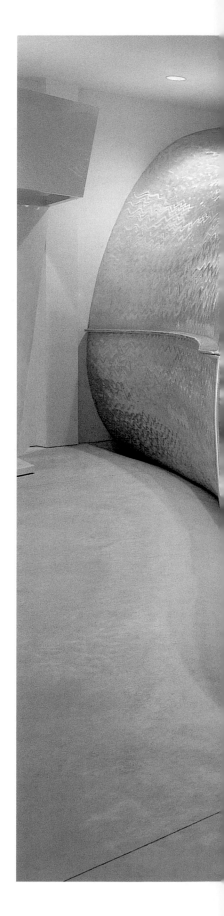

right The metal entrance tunnel is made entirely of aluminium. The vast tube was constructed in a boat-builder's workshop in Cornwall before being shipped to New York.

HADI TEHERANI
CAR SHOWROOM, HAMBURG, 1991

Set in a no-man's land of factories and offices on the outskirts of Hamburg, this new showroom for luxury cars adjoins a workshop for their restoration and conversion. An existing building was remodelled to accommodate the workshop, and a striking new sales area and showroom for a range of exclusive marques (including Bentley, Rolls-Royce and Lagonda) was added as the focus of the development. This is a simple rectangular box with three glazed walls. Despite its relatively modest size, this unobtrusive glass box transforms a prosaic brief into a bold and brilliant formal gesture. The building has become the company's trademark, providing a sense of discreet glamour.

The fourth side, along the building line of the existing sheds, is closed. Angled asymmetrically towards the entrance, the main façade draws people in towards the building. It also tilts forwards, improving views and preventing glare and reflections. Running along the edge of the glass wall is a shallow pool which forms a moat around the building that is crossed by a gently sloping drawbridge clad in slats of timber, with a metal balustrade. Protected by a red zigzag roof resembling an angular tongue, the drawbridge marks the entrance. The roof is suspended by a network of tensile wires, so that it appears to hover above the bridge. Doors are simple sheets of clear glass set in a recessed vertical wall. The tension between the angled façade and the funnelled approach sets up a dynamic effect, emphasizing a sense of movement.

The diaphanous glass façade consists of a planar glazing system, with loads transferred through pairs of scissor-shaped steel arms to inclined tubular steel columns. With its rigging and mast-like columns, the wall explores an aesthetic borrowed from yachts and marine technology. The notion of a drawbridge is unusual, in that its purpose is generally to provide protection and defence. Here, the traditional role is subverted and the bridge is designed to channel people into the showroom: it welcomes customers, as opposed to repelling unwanted visitors.

At the time of the building's completion, in the early 1990s, the construction of such a lightweight glazed façade was quite novel in Hamburg, where the predominant material is brick. Obviously informed and inspired by the British High Tech movement, Teherani's architecture exudes precision and refinement, but is ultimately subservient to the building's function – the selling of wonderfully sleek cars.

left *The bold red canopy and timber bridge slicing through the delicate glass façade leaves visitors in no doubt as to where to enter the building.*

113

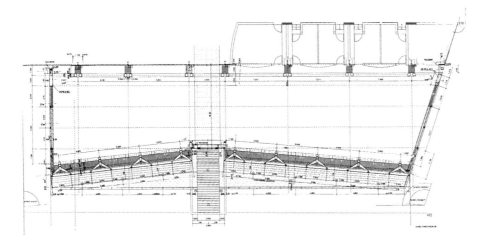

Floor plan

above left *The canopy appears to hang tenuously from the roof, attached by a network of steel tension cables.*

above right *A moat along the entry façade heightens the tension between inside and out, and gives even greater importance to the bridge as the only point at which the building can be accessed.*

right *The zigzag canopy continues into the main car display area where it creates a dialogue with the V-shaped metal glazing struts.*

DILLER + SCOFIDIO
THE BRASSERIE, NEW YORK, 2000

Located in the Seagram Building, Mies van der Rohe's iconic Modernist tower, The Brasserie has been given a striking makeover by the New York-based partnership of Diller + Scofidio. The restaurant in the base of the tower fell victim to a fire in the mid-1990s. Diller + Scofidio were commissioned to remodel and revitalize it and have created an interior that plays intriguing perceptual games through subtle curves, tilts, textures and layering.

The revamp opens up the room as a dramatic primary space, elevating the act of dining into a public performance. This is definitely not a place for a clandestine rendezvous. The most prominent feature is a warped skin that envelopes the main dining area. The madrone floor peels up to join a pearwood ceiling which peels down and is moulded into seating creating a rippling lining that serves not just as an aesthetic device, but as a spatial and structural element. A sense of theatricality and illusion pervades the interior, but particular ingenuity is expended on the sequence of entry. The minute diners swing through the doors at street level, their arrival is recorded by a tiny camera triggered by a sensor in the front door. The images are fed to a row of fifteen video screens mounted above the bar, where a freeze-frame tableau of these pivotal moments is on display for the scrutiny of those already seated. Once through the white terrazzo lobby deck, prospective diners descend into the full gaze of the assembled throng, down a glass staircase that resembles an ultra-modern gangplank and whose attenuated shallow steps make each newly-arriving guest as on display as any catwalk model.

The splicing and reconstitution of time and space coupled with the elevation of voyeurism from an act of surreptitious surveillance into one of social celebration are characteristic Diller + Scofidio gestures. In this case, the profusion of gestures and ideas is at times daunting, but the rippling polished timber skin gives the interior a spatial and formal coherence. Cool, chic and clinical, this is without doubt the restaurant to be seen in. It also revives a historic structure with skill and inventiveness, although Elizabeth Diller is refreshingly downbeat about the achievement: "We thought of the space we inherited as an old coat that just needed a new lining."

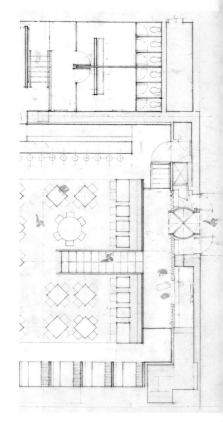

Floor plan

left *Closed-circuit monitors above the bar in the restaurant relay pictures of diners progressing from the entrance at street level through the angled timber shell and down the glass staircase.*

right *Entering the dining room via the glass stair puts guests on show for the voyeuristic benefit of their fellow diners.*

EDUARDO SOUTO DE MOURA
POUSADA DE SANTA MARIA, BRAGA, 1997

Since the 1940s, an array of historic Portuguese buildings – medieval castles, Renaissance palaces, Baroque monasteries and disused convents – have been converted into small, state-run luxury hotels known as *pousadas*. Scattered throughout Portugal, these remodelled relics form a network that supports culturally based tourism and helps to maintain a precious architectural heritage that might otherwise be lost through decay and obsolescence.

Eduardo Souto de Moura's restoration of the Cistercian monastery of Santa Maria do Bouro shows how a historic structure can be sensitively brought back to life. Founded in 1162, the monastery has been rebuilt several times; the present building dates back to the eighteenth century and is attached to a church still in use. Today, the Pousada de Santa Maria serves visitors to the ancient northern city of Braga, a religious centre renowned for its historic churches and Easter week processions. When Souto de Moura began work, the building was an overgrown ruin: little remained but its crumbling walls. He decided to make the ruin habitable, using modern means, but with a clear respect for the remains, an approach consistent with the evolution of the monastery complex over the last eight centuries, in which buildings were manipulated and transformed to serve new functions.

The *pousada's* thirty-three rooms are arranged around two open spaces: a U-shaped courtyard planted with orange trees; and a cloister restored as a freestanding circuit of arcade walls. Guest rooms are austere modern equivalents of monks' cells. The former kitchen has become a dining room, its massive pyramidal brick chimney transformed into a monumental skylight. A new service wing was built against the lower flanks of the south façade, its roof acting as a terrace for the public rooms off the cloister. A tennis court and small oval swimming pool discreetly nestle in the semi-wild grounds, which retain their ancient paths and stone walls.

Souto de Moura won the commission largely because of his experience with traditional stonework. To repair and stabilize the walls, he introduced a series of minimal, carefully constructed elements, such as the exposed steel deck that replaces the roof. Door and window openings are precisely detailed, with brass frames that are virtually invisible from the outside. External doors are made from angled sections of pre-rusted steel, forming gridded planes that blend with the existing architecture and permit views through the cloisters and courtyards. Throughout, Souto de Moura's resolution of the problem of containing modern comfortable lodgings within an older, spartan structure seems natural and effortless, giving history a new lease of life.

above *At the termination of a three-sided courtyard planted with a grid of orange trees, a stone archway heralds the entrance to the hotel lobby.*

Section and elevation

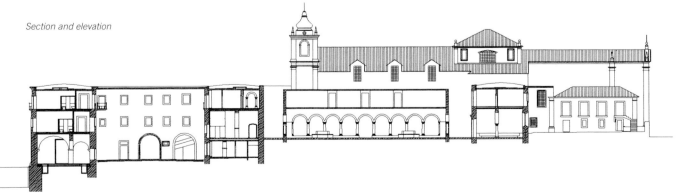

119

left *Sensitive contemporary detailing, such as this pivoting door, preserve the integrity of the old stone-work, seen here in the arcaded cloister.*

above left and right *The corridors leading to the guest rooms retain the dignified simplicity of the monastic architecture.*

PHILIPPE STARCK
ST MARTIN'S LANE HOTEL, LONDON, 1999

After realizing a string of modish boutique hotels in America, entrepreneur Ian Schrager has turned his sights on London. Working as usual with iconoclastic French designer Philippe Starck, one of Schrager's latest ventures is St Martin's Lane Hotel, located on the cusp of London's theatreland. The 1960s office block has been transformed by Starck into an entrancing demi-monde of colour and light that sparkles with his characteristic wit and taste for the grand gesture.

The tone of delightful discovery is set at the hotel entrance, which faces onto bustling St Martin's Lane. A three-quarter length pale blue net curtain screens the interior behind the clear glass façade. Below, a succession of busy legs can be seen marching up and down. Set into the façade is an oversized revolving door, made of vivid yellow panes of glass that seem to glow with light. At 4.5m (14½ ft) high, it is said to be the largest in Europe and its Brobdingnagian proportions suggest that all is not as it seems. At night the door's giant cylindrical form is emphasized by pools of light. Like Alice gingerly stepping into Wonderland, you enter. The door glides smoothly on its central pivot and delivers you into the tall space of the main lobby. Bright yellow fluorescent walls, punctuated by underlit columns open up this public part of the hotel. An asymmetrical carpet of light projected onto a sleek limestone floor beckons you to a far video wall that shimmers and pulsates. Fat columns subdivide the lobby into seating and reception areas. Spaces between the columns each have distinct characters, created by the play of light and choice of furniture that includes gold stools fashioned like molar teeth, long steel benches upholstered with pink padded silk, kitschy garden gnomes and hand-carved stools from the Philippines. While this surreal ensemble might seem visually overwhelming, the effect is not overdone, partly because the giant columns prevent you from taking in the *bricolage* at a glance. Instead, they are set pieces to be discovered episodically, as you move through the lobby.

"This is the first modern hotel," Starck asserts. "Modernity is transparency, energy and dematerialization. We played with light and colour to give it life. We wanted a boiling pot with all the energy of the city." Across the threshold of the giant revolving door, Starck's mixture of whimsy, energy and serenity redefines the notion of the designer hotel.

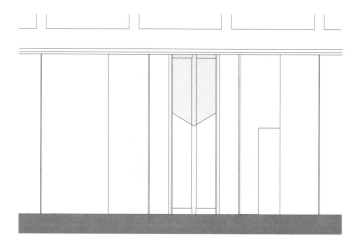

Exterior elevation

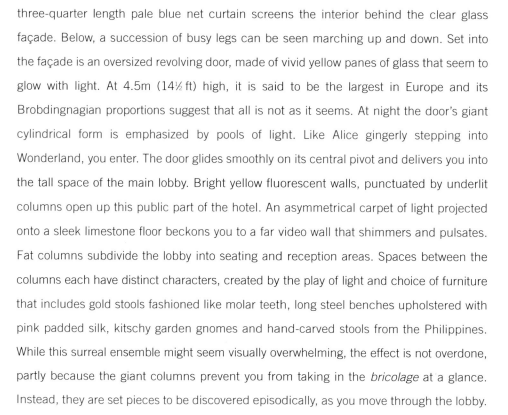

right *From the street, the entrance to the hotel is surprisingly modest, but warm lights within entice the guest through the massive revolving glass doors towards the bars and restaurant.*

HERZOG & DE MEURON
KÜPPERSMÜHLE MUSEUM, GROTHE COLLECTION, DUISBURG, 1999

The Küppersmühle in Duisburg is a striking city landmark and the most historically significant structure in Duisburg's inner harbour, an area currently being rejuvenated to a masterplan by Norman Foster. A key part of this plan involves finding new uses for industrial antiquities such as the Küppersmühle. Herzog & de Meuron were asked to convert the building to house Hans Grothe's collection of post-war German art.

Three floors of galleries are linked by a new stair tower, placed to the rear of the main warehouse block. The stark lines of the tower echo the Küppersmühle's muscular, industrial functionalism. Narrow strips of vertical glazing are incised with surgical precision into the tower's terracotta-coloured concrete flanks. Existing windows in the part of the warehouse housing the galleries have been sealed up using bricks of the same colour and texture of the original walls. This muting of the façade heightens the building's monolithic, elemental character and gives the new elements a singular and surprising intensity. The main entrance is a wide glazed slot inserted into the brickwork, like a shop window. The truncated cylinder of a revolving door, a solid geometrical presence, marks the point of public entry. Beside the glazed slot is the loading bay for bringing artworks into the building. Usually this disregarded, workaday element is kept well out of public view; but here it is gloriously celebrated. The tall door is clad in horizontal strips of burnished copper which scintillate like fish scales.

Inside, a sinuous stair winds up to the exhibition spaces, creating a logical and leisurely promenade through the building. Galleries are calm spaces, with simple white walls and cool stone floors. Some daylight is admitted through a handful of carefully positioned glazed strips. Herzog & de Meuron's strategy of intervention and renewal seeks to respect both the building and its contents. The Grothe Collection has a handsome new home with all the technical and cultural amenities of a modern art museum and the Küppersmühle has acquired a dynamic new lease of life.

above *The rawness of the in-situ concrete staircase in the entry space complements the monumental insular quality of the converted brick warehouse into which it has been inserted.*

left *Thin strip windows allow a controlled quantity of daylight into the new gallery spaces, while the existing windows have been bricked up with masonry that is the same colour and texture as the existing walls.*

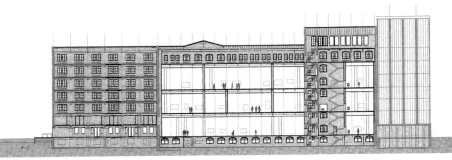

Exterior elevation

TRANSITIONS
& THRESHOLDS

In mythology, doors and gates traditionally mark the threshold between the different worlds, and art and literature abound with fables of guardians, gatekeepers and rites of passage. A door represents mystery, alluding to unknown forces and powers on its other side. Many examples of rituals and beliefs associated with entrances can be divined from ancient civilizations through to the present day. Although architecture is rooted in reality and must perform certain practical functions, the physical expression of transition from public to private, from inside to outside, from light to dark has always presented fertile scope for designers' imaginations. The entry sequence to Tadao Ando's Buddhist temple, for instance, marks the portal between the secular world and the realm of the divine. As the projects in this concluding chapter demonstrate, the threshold remains one of architecture's most potent moments.

right *The expression of transition from different realms, from public to private, from inside to outside, from sacred to profane has always presented fertile scope for designers' imaginations. View through the opening to the Oulart Monument in County Wexford, Ireland, by Scott Tallon Walker.*

TADAO ANDO
HONKPUKU-JI WATER TEMPLE, AWAJI-SHIMA, 1991

The work of Japanese architect Tadao Ando embraces a contemplative, ascetic realm of stillness and abstraction. Monastic in their rigour, his buildings embody a rare mastery of light and materials that seeks to reconnect mankind with nature. As a child, he came into contact with the great classics of *minka* (farm buildings) and historic Japanese *sukiya* architecture. Yet the outcome of this influence is not a slavish recreation of vernacular forms or styles. To his austere buildings Ando brings *genus loci*, or spirit of place, that explores and responds to the individual qualities and regional vernacular of each site.

In form, materials and processional sequence, Ando's Honkpuku-ji Water Temple in Awaji-shima, Japan, is far removed from traditional timber temple structures. The temple hall is underground, beneath a large oval pool filled with floating lotus plants which signify the enlightened soul rising from the world's corruptions. Expressed as an impassive, enigmatic volume in the landscape, the pool is enclosed by curved concrete walls of exquisite smoothness. The entrance is a carefully considered promenade, rich in allegory and symbolism. The subterranean sanctuary is reached by a narrow stair sliced across the short axis of the elliptical pool. Visitors process down the long staircase below the level of the water, an original inversion of the traditional ascent to a conventional temple. The physical and sensory compression of the narrow staircase screens out the world in preparation for entering the realm of the numinous. A simple door at the bottom of the staircase leads into the temple's inner sanctum.

The shape of the pool is extended below ground as the building's defining form. Roughly half the ellipse contains a circular temple sanctuary, formed by a wall of tightly lapped Japanese cypress boards painted rich vermilion, a traditional Buddhist colour. Columns and gridded timber screens enclosing the statue of Amida Buddha are also an intense red. This is the first use of strong hue in Ando's aesthetically monochromatic architecture and it creates the illusion of a vermilion volume where the air seems to be saturated with colour. Natural light is admitted behind the shrine through windows in the exposed retaining wall. Discovering light after descending underground magnifies the temple's sense of sacred drama and mystery. Typical of Ando's buildings, the temple is a microcosmic enclave of tranquillity in which water and mass, colour and light, artifice and nature are combined in exquisite harmony.

right *The entry slices across the lily-covered pool, descending into the subterranean enclosure of the chapel.*

above left *From above, the simplicity and clarity of the architectural concept is even more apparent. The symmetrical arrangement imposes a strong sense of order onto the processional route into the chapel.*

above right *Visitors experience the unusual sensation of walking down the steps, past the water line, apparently disappearing into the pool.*

right *Looking up the staircase, along the beautiful smoothness of the concrete walls, a trademark of Ando's work, creates a striking linear vista upward towards the sky.*

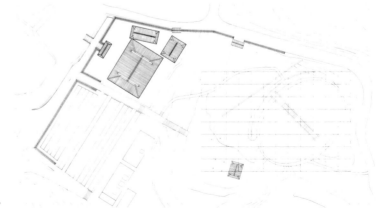

Site plan

UN STUDIO
BRIDGE CONTROL CENTRE, PURMEREND, 1998

left *The small door to the Bridge Control Centre is set back into the perforated metal mesh that sheaths the entire building.*

right *Set on a plinth, hovering above the water, the light from within the building shimmers out through the fine-mesh cladding.*

Full of rivers, tributaries and canals, the landscape of The Netherlands is also full of the attendant trappings of water management. The design of these technological objects involves architects in the unglamorous territory of civil engineering, but connections between architects and engineers must be strengthened if the appearance of infrastructural buildings is to be improved. This little project shows that such generally neglected objects can still embody a tough, tectonic lyricism and make a positive contribution to their surroundings.

Now working as part of UN Studio, Ben van Berkel and Caroline Bos have a reputation for making ruggedly poetic structures out of uncompromising industrial and infrastructural programmes. This recent project for a bridge control centre at Purmerend deftly elaborates on a basic brief to create a strong sculptural presence in the flat polder landscape. The bridge is made up of three separate, parallel roadways that open and close asynchronously, as if imitating the movement of fingers playing a keyboard. This intricate sequence is controlled from a bridgekeeper's station housed in a tapering, slab-like volume set on an adjacent jetty. The bridgekeeper occupies two upper storeys hoisted aloft on a chunky, inclined podium. Technical facilities are at ground level, with living quarters and an operations room above. A visor-like window for the control centre at the uppermost level is incised into the width of the structure. This and a small door at its base are the building's only extraneous articulation. Almost domestic in scale, the door is set back from the line of the external walls and an angular canopy lined with blue-tinted glass marks the point of entry. Like the entire building, the doorway exudes an air of intrigue.

The simple concrete form of the building is sheathed in panels of finely perforated steel mesh which lend it a curious ethereality, particularly at night, when light gently diffuses through the lower, eroded portion of the structure so that the building appears to hover above the water. The mesh generates a shimmering *moiré* effect, like silk, its lightness dematerializing the monolithic mass of the structure.

Exterior elevation

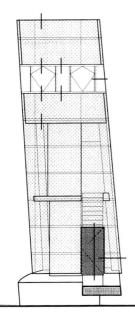

STEVEN HOLL
ST IGNATIUS CHAPEL, SEATTLE, 1995

Its fluid spaces animated by an exquisite combination of direct and diffuse light, the Chapel of St Ignatius by Steven Holl uses illumination as a powerful metaphor for spiritual life. Conceived as a metaphorical gathering of different lights, the building is a quiet reminder that meaning is still possible in architecture.

Located at Seattle University, a private Jesuit-run college of around 6,000 students, the chapel is carefully sited to define four new quadrangles in a developing area of this urban campus. For the external walls, Holl used a system of reinforced concrete panels, which were cast on site and then put into position by cranes. Each shaped differently and irregularly, the slabs fit together like pieces of a puzzle, with window openings situated at interlocking points. The concrete is finished with an ochre-coloured stain reminiscent of ancient Italian churches and the whole is crowned with a sculptural zinc-clad roof.

At the south end is the main entrance to the chapel, an imposing door of thick Alaskan cedar. It is of double form, but the panels are of slightly different sizes, emphasizing the building's poetic irregularities. Oval apertures are cut at random into the timber, so that light can percolate through the door, especially at night. Handles are made of cast-bronze strips, curved and bent like rough strips of ribbon. The heaviness and coldness of the bronze contrast with the warmth of the wood.

The fluid, aqueous spaces of earlier Holl projects are developed here into a rich complex interior, which is a built metaphor of spiritual life. The concept of gathering of different lights governs the design of the interior. Six light scoops, each a different shape and each facing a different direction, admit light into the calm, luminous space. Expressed in one of Holl's original watercolour renderings as "bottles of light," the idea expresses the doctrines of St Ignatius, which aimed at attaining communion with the sacred realm.

The tactile qualities of the materials in the chapel – rough plaster, cast glass, hewn wood and gold leaf – are quietly compelling. Visitors are drawn to touch these surfaces, not casually, but slowly and with reverence. Indeed, the richest aspect of the intertwining of sensory stimuli with both experience and imagination is the degree to which the craft of the human hand is revealed. Together with the explicit iconography of Catholicism, the building, which reveals the texture of the trowel, the irregularity of blown glass and the mark of the chisel, presents another iconography – of the human potential to create beauty with imperfection. That is surely an inspiration for all who enter.

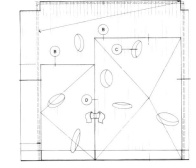

Exterior elevation

right *The focal point for the chapel is the main door and entranceway. Steven Holl has produced a modern version of the church door, which traditionally featured elaborate ornamentation, by carving random oval shapes out of the thick cedar panels.*

left *Inside, Holl uses surfaces of varying textures to amplify the qualities of natural light in a way that is essential to how the chapel is perceived by its users.*

above left *The different sizes of the two leaves that make up the double doors communicates the idea of earth-based imperfection and irregularity that Holl incorporated into the design.*

above right *The chapel's bell tower above the main door is reflected in the pool below, adding to the dynamic drama created by the light pouring out of the varying oval shapes cut into the wood.*

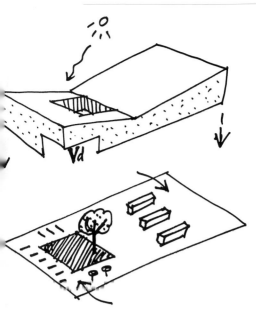

NEUTELINGS RIEDIJK
VEENMAN PRINTERS, EDE, 1997

Schematic design sketch

left *The printing company's logo is used on a gigantic scale to support the corner of the building and to signal the location of the entry.*

below *The glass façade, printed with simple sans serif letters, continues the typographical theme from the entry to all surfaces of the building.*

Set on a dull industrial estate on the outskirts of Ede in the Netherlands, Neutelings Riedjik's complex for Veenman Drukkers, an arts-based print company, elevates the functional typography of the printworks to often theatrical heights of invention.

The doughnut-plan form is enclosed by a gently sloping V-shaped roof rising from the two-storey office over the print shop and storage areas. From the nearby motorway, the building's V-shaped profile (a sly abstraction of Veenman's corporate logo) is a conspicuous presence. The logo is repeated more explicitly in the superscale letters that support and signal the main entrance, which is cut into the building's south-west corner. As if revealing a rich, inner layer, the cut sections of wall are clad in vivid blue panels.

The most striking use of graphics, however, is on the exterior. Above a base of dark-grey concrete blocks, the building is wrapped in a skin of panes of clear glass which are set slightly forward from a white reflective membrane that encloses an insulation layer behind. Between glass and membrane is a ventilated cavity. Appropriating greenhouse construction methods, panes of cheap, durable glass are set in glazing bars supported by horizontal rails. Edging the panes with black rubber strips helps to break down the scale of the façade.

The glass forms an ideal printing surface and is used to realize the building's primary artistic conceit. Each pane is printed with a single black letter 1m (3ft) high, designed by typographer Karel Martens. Together they make up a specially commissioned poem (musing on the sun, wind and sky) by Dutch writer Karl Schippers. It is impossible to discern where the text ends and begins, and this, coupled with the absence of punctuation and words turned around corners, serves to heighten the surreal ambiguity of the message. The building becomes a piece of text, and the subtly changing shadows cast by the alphabetic panels on the white membrane give the façade an enlivening depth and animation, intensifying the sense of theatre. Informed by an astute concern for materials and construction, Neutelings Riedijk's witty, perplexing building makes literal and architectural poetry out of a potentially prosaic programme.

139

ARCHITECTURE STUDIO
NOTRE DAME DE L'ARCHE D'ALLIANCE, PARIS, 1998

Reflecting the progress within Catholicism towards a less rigidly formal spirit of worship, Architecture Studio's parish church in Paris explores the nature of modern sacred space in an urban context. Churchgoing is declining in France and it was hoped that the new building would swell the congregation and encourage more young people to attend.

Set in a neighbourhood of rather soulless post-war tower blocks, the Church of Our Lady of the Ark of the Covenant is an exercise in geometrical and biblical allusion. Based on the exact proportions of a cube, the main volume of the church is elevated on twelve cylindrical *piloti*, representing both the Apostles and the Tribes of Israel. The *piloti* and the overhanging volume form a cloister which connects with an austerely landscaped square on the north-east side of the church.

Chosen for its symbolic associations (equal sides reflecting God's omnipresence), the cubic form also alludes to the Ark of the Covenant. Both church and Ark embody the notion of a sacred vessel or box (in the Old Testament, the gold-plated chest of the Ark represented the presence of God for the Jewish people). The cube is clad in finely jointed terracotta-coloured cladding panels, some stencilled with the text of *Ave Maria*. Printed in gold, the angelic salutation, which is repeated as a chant, poem, incantation and prayer, helps to dematerialize the massive, inert volume of the cube. This sense of dematerialization is emphasized by a three-dimensional metal grid that encloses the cube, like a huge cage. The stainless-steel structure creates a transition between the secular world and the sanctuary of the church. On the south-east face, a spindly steel-framed cylinder hung with bells (an abstraction of a traditional campanile), soars above the surrounding roofs.

The skeletal campanile also marks the entrance to the church. Simple double doors, executed in the same material as the walls, lead into a small vestibule and the inner sanctum beyond. Like an exquisitely crafted cabinet, the symmetrical volume of the nave is lined with dark wood panels. A black slate floor reinforces the building's austere materiality. Spiral staircases enclosed by minimal glass balustrades set at the corners of the cube wind up to galleries at the upper levels, and light from stained-glass clerestories inscribed with biblical texts gently washes the interior.

To evoke the other-worldly often requires a rigour and intensity. Although Architecture Studio's geometric tactics are highly Mannerist (in the best French tradition), the stark cube has a curious potency: it is a modern Ark for a modern parish, sheltering the sacred and symbolizing the meeting of God and mankind.

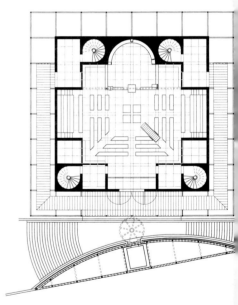

Ground floor plan

right *The unusually thick double-entry doors, clad in the same material as the façade, emphasizes the solidity and permanence the church represents.*

left *The cylindrical campanile, towering above the streets of Paris, is flanked at ground level by a broad double stair climbing up to the entrance from both sides of the building.*

above *In the interior, the formal grid that defines the cubic form of the building, continues to cut through the top-lit space of the chapel.*

Exterior elevation

143

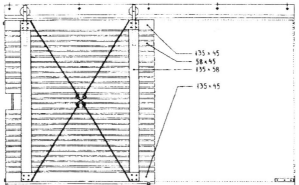

135 × 45
58 × 45
135 × 58

135 × 45

Detail of door assembly

CARL-VIGGIO HØLMBAKK
CREMATORIUM MORTUARY, ASKER, 1999

His works may so far only be relatively small scale, but the young Norwegian architect Carl-Viggo Hølmebakk has acquired a reputation for creating architecture of great formal and material sensitivity. Commissioned to design an addition to a crematorium in the small town of Asker, on the western outskirts of Oslo in Norway, Hølmebakk has responded with a building that is modest yet endowed with characteristic grace and subtlety. The existing crematorium dates from the 1950s and Hølmebakk was asked to make a new mortuary annexe consisting of three main spaces – a coffin-receiving room, a room for the preparation of the corpse and an outdoor court. The small entrance area connecting the mortuary to the existing building now serves as a place where the urn can be handed over to relatives after the cremation.

Hølmebakk's set of simple, austere spaces tenderly responds to the rituals of death. The deceased is brought to the main entrance and taken into the receiving room. Here, relatives can spend final moments with the dead person prior to cremation, which takes place in the main building. Attached to the receiving room is a preparation room, normally used by undertakers, but which is also accessible to family members who want to take part in the preparation of the body. A curved wall encloses an external courtyard that functions as a quiet, contemplative outdoor room. A wild cherry tree planted in the courtyard will eventually create a sheltering roof of branches.

The courtyard is separated and screened from the parking area by a sliding door, which enables the main door to the receiving room to remain open during the ceremony while preserving a degree of privacy. Made of horizontal slats of Norwegian pine treated with a glossy oil, the sliding door is precisely and elegantly detailed. Slim steel rods form cross-bracing and the handle is a simple stainless steel tube. The main door to the receiving room is also made of oiled pine, its warmth and tactile nature forming a counterpoint to the clinical white brick of the walls and the terrazzo and marble floors. Fittings for the lighting and candles are made of sandblasted stainless steel.

Even though the building makes no conventional references to religion, many features seem to be metaphors for some kind of relationship with the numinous. The proportions of the rooms, the geometry, the soft light filtered from above, the fixtures, the slatted-screen door, the sequence of entry – even the texture of the terrazzo floors – all seem to have symbolic meaning. These features, however, are also part of a wider Nordic building tradition in which architecture acts as a catalyst of social and spiritual consciousness.

above *Set beneath an inverted L-shaped canopy, the slatted timber door continues the horizontality of the slim stretcher bond brickwork.*

145

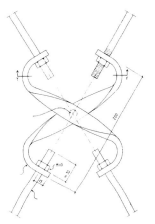

Detail of cross-bracing to door

above left The simple austerity of the interior creates an appropriately sombre environment in which the bereaved are able to spent their last moments with the deceased.

above right The elegantly expressive steel cross-bracing on the doors lends a decorative flourish to the otherwise rational simplicity of the building.

right The enclosed courtyard, with its single cherry tree, functions as a quiet contemplative space for the mourners.

RICHARD ROGERS
CHANNEL FOUR HEADQUARTERS, LONDON, 1994

At its inception in the early 1980s, the independent television company Channel 4 occupied a disparate collection of buildings in central London. By 1990, the company had decided to consolidate its television studios, post-production facilities and offices in a single complex, so a limited competition was held to find a suitable design. The Richard Rogers Partnership won with a scheme that makes a provocative urban statement in a part of London dominated by dull Civil Service offices and nondescript mansion blocks.

A conscious set piece of urban theatre, the building exploits its tight corner site by means of a relatively simple plan; two four-storey wings containing offices above ground and studios below are joined together at right angles by a knuckle of circulation. Their union is consummated by a concave glass wall, dramatically suspended from a delicate network of stainless steel rods and cables. Terminating either end of the piazza-like space created by the corner's recess are sentinel towers, which contain lifts and meeting rooms and are topped with bristling satellite dishes and plant machinery.

The sequence of entry is particularly dramatic. Shallow curved steps rise up from the pavement to connect with a glazed, umbilical bridge that leads to the main entrance. The bridge traverses a circular moat giving unexpected views through an oculus of the preview theatre's foyer below. A steel and glass canopy thrusts out like a suggestive, protecting tongue over the bridge and a pair of cylindrical revolving doors mark the point of entry.

With its tiers of cantilevered walkways and steel roof structure, the four-storey entrance atrium forms the building's spectacular transparent hub. From here there are tantalizing glimpses into the staff canteen, which is half a level down, and through to the tranquil green courtyard at the heart of the complex. On the upper levels, the curved link between the two office wings contains executive suites, some of which face into the atrium, while on the top floor there is a directors' terrace.

In a signature Rogers' move, fixed elements of circulation and services are extruded from the central volume. This creates flexible interior spaces and breaks down the scale of the building using the dissection of its various elements in an almost decorative, Mannerist way. It also anchors the building firmly in the streetscape by announcing its use and exposing its inner workings through the vertical traffic of the lift capsules and the constant human animation of the pivotal entrance atrium. In its highly inventive use of space, technology and materials, the Channel 4 building is another manifestation of Rogers' long-standing concern to make buildings that contribute and respond to the life of the city.

right The slender suspended glass canopy projects out over a circular cut in the ground, which is traversed by a bridge that connects the street to the entry.

Section through entry

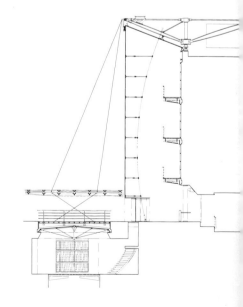

left *Looking out through the glass atrium, the dominating symmetry of the forecourt is bisected by the tongue of the entrance canopy.*

above left *The entrance space is dominated by the layers of mezzanine office floors stacked up around the curved glass façade.*

above right *A typical Rogers urban gesture: a tower with circulation, services, plant and communication equipment signals the entry to the building.*

JOHN WINTER
INSIGNIA HOUSE, LONDON, 1990

Mansell Street occupies a curious hinterland where the City of London meets the East End. Within this relatively short geographical distance, the changes in scale and urban character are peculiarly abrupt, best exemplified by the spectacle of raffish street markets lapping around the beached whales of corporate monuments. A busy, noisy thoroughfare, Mansell Street is not a place to linger.

The street has been gradually remodelled and the existing building stock replaced with a succession of plodding exercises in pre-packaged medium-rise office space. One exception to this is an infill block designed by John Winter in collaboration with Elana Keats. It suggests ways of using modern technology to set up new relationships between exterior and interior and, in doing so, proposes a more inspiring form of urban commercial architecture.

The building conforms to the irregular rectangular footprint left by the site's original occupant, a light industrial warehouse. The office space is arranged on six floors that are dramatically enclosed on the street frontage by a glass box which acts like a huge display cabinet. This glazed void acts as a thermal and acoustic buffer, screening working areas from the din of traffic. It also creates animation and intimacy at street level. Public and semi-public areas are separated by the thinnest sliver of planar glazing, transforming the entrance hall into a human goldfish bowl. The atrium reaches out to connect and engage with the street, thereby demystifying the building and its function.

Consisting of two steel masts pin jointed at the top and bottom with horizontal bracing at two-metre (6.5 ft) intervals, the glass wall is a tautly detailed exercise in technical expression. Sheets of 10mm (⅜in) thick armour-plated glass are held in place by a system of glazing cleats connected to steel lugs, welded at intervals to the horizontal booms. Additional bracing is provided by adjustable steel tension wires.

The entrance is a glazed cube set in the wall, with two sets of double doors to create a draught lobby. The floor and reception desk are covered in sinuously veined, dark-green slate, its leaden matt texture a thoughtful antidote to the ostentatious sheen of marble more usually associated with such spaces. On one side of the atrium a glass elevator whizzes up and down, giving vertiginous views over the City. The building is a theatrical joy on this dreary street, especially at night when its glowing light fills the space.

above *Standing in the entrance lobby, the glass-enclosed sliver of space between the street and the offices towers up the entire six-storey height of the building.*

right *The glass maintains a continuously smooth surface across the external surface of the façade.*

Exterior elevation

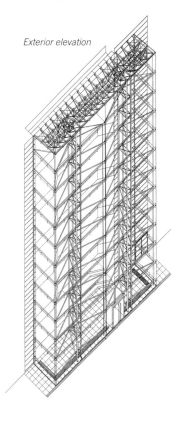

MIRALLES & TAGLIABUE
JUGENDMUSIKSCHULE, HAMBURG, 1998

Designed by Barcelona-based partnership of Enric Miralles and Benedetta Tagliabue, the Jugendmusikschule lies in one of Hamburg's most luxurious leafy inner-city neighbourhoods. Professional music tuition is part of the state school system and, with an opera and various professional orchestras and choirs to run, Hamburg is keen to foster local talent. Architecture is often described as "frozen music", but here it comes vividly to life.

Miralles' early sketches for the competition, which his office won in 1997, played with the idea of a concert piano. The resulting elevations retain keyboard associations, for instance there is a flying auditorium wing with a composer's studio to one side that looks like the bulbous curve of a grand piano in plan. The trees on the site define the framework of the project and tree-like crowns form roofs. Vividly coloured concrete and steel columns merge with the planting to create a forest pattern of trunks. Swaying branches and leaves are set against concrete, red-brown brickwork, glass, and grey and kaleidoscopic steel. Different textures and colours form a patchwork. This counterpoint rhythm of natural and man-made elements alludes to music, both classical and modern.

A freestanding curved concrete wall and mature chestnut trees shield the school from a busy main road. Behind this screen the three-storey building is reached through a boomerang-shaped foyer of sloping steel and glazed walls. Entry is through a skewed canopy supported on groups of splayed steel columns, with doors that have windows at child's eye level (a characteristically thoughtful touch). The entrance has a powerful yet inviting sculptural quality and is the pivotal point of the school. The café and lecture rooms lead directly off the foyer, while the approach to the first-floor auditorium – a wide ramp like staircase – acts as a proscenium for formal addresses at public performances.

Two floors of open galleries rise above the foyer, transforming the musicians carrying instruments between classes, into walk-on extras in a theatre production. Sound is well dampened and only the occasional flute, violin or oboe can be heard only when a door is opened. From the galleries, corridors meander off into the outstretched wings of administration, classrooms and practice rooms, where the mood becomes more introverted and concentrated. Architecture has a calculated effect on creativity, and it will be intriguing to see what impact this freely designed, colourful and generously articulated environment will have on a new generation of musicians.

left *A forest of tilted circular steel columns props up an entrance canopy whose geometry is inspired by the lid of a grand piano.*

159

left The pattern of the glazing on the façades, the roof and the entrance canopy have been designed to resemble piano keys.

above left At the rear of the building, a system of covered ramps and walkways elevated above the ground continues the dynamic expression used throughout the design.

Design sketch

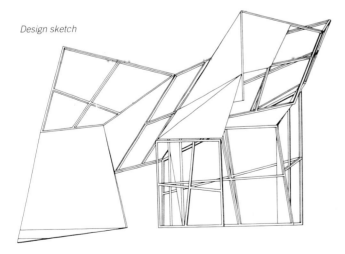

above A curved concrete wall formally frames the glazed entrance and acts as a buffer between the busy city and the necessary quiet needed for the musicians to practice and perform.

ERIK VAN EGERAAT
COLLEGE OF FASHION & GRAPHICS, UTRECHT, 1997

The College of Fashion and Graphics is the most recent addition to Utrecht's technical college. Located on a sprawling suburban campus, it comprises three low-rise horizontal blocks cranked around a courtyard. The largest block contains cellular classrooms, linked to an interstitial wing housing a canteen and theatre. A third, smaller part containing facilities for a Montessori school meets the ancillary link at an obtuse angle.

The project had an unconventional gestation. The original proposal from Utrecht's own building department was rejected by the local review panel and the head of the building department called on Erick van Egeraat to devise a more acceptable architectural solution. Work on the project was far advanced, so van Egeraat had to accept the constraints of the original three-storey building form. He built the school largely as initially proposed, but then sheathed it in a delicately transparent external skin, which affirmed the building's independence from the original design and transformed the dull college blocks into objects of fascination and intrigue. Van Egeraat compares the glass envelope to a gauze veil, simultaneously concealing and revealing; a metaphor for the tantalizing vicissitudes of fashion.

Van Egeraat had a relatively free hand in the north-east corner, where the orthogonal plan is fractured to create a luminous entrance atrium, which is also an exhibition space. The triple-height volume is enclosed by a glass screen wall and glazed roof. Within the atrium is a small theatre, clad in translucent, ribbed fibreglass panels. Elevated on a random grid of spindly, angular *pilotis*, the cuboid volume of the theatre is linked to classrooms and ancillary spaces by glazed bridges that create a sense of procession and arrival. The doors to the theatre are simple plywood panels – opaque insertions in the translucent wall. The underside of the theatre box is also clad in smooth plywood sheets.

The complex layering and fracturing of the semi-public atrium and theatre spaces contrast with the ordered ranks of classrooms in the teaching blocks. Light diffuses through the theatre's translucent cladding, infusing the surrounding atrium with a surreal, radioactive glow; a further variation on the continually surprising play of light and materials.

above An overhead bridge cutting through the entrance space crashes at an angle into the freestanding theatre, placed as a box within the box of the main space.

right From inside the clear glazed frame of the main space, the theatre, set on a collection of angular pilotis, glows luminously.

Section

BAUMSCHLAGER & EBERLE
SIRCH TIMBER WAREHOUSE AND WORKSHOP, BÖHEN, 1998

Certain regional factors have come to exert a strong influence on the work of the young Austrian partnership of Carlo Baumschlager and Dietmar Eberle. Based in the western Vorarlberg region, Austria's smallest and, after Vienna, most densely populated region, the partnership draws on local rural traditions of carpentry and woodworking, allied to a mentality of thriftiness. Here timidity about public ostentation still persists. Notions of simplicity, rationality and suitability are applied by the pair in a pragmatic and economical way that has attracted both public and private sector clients.

Since the mid-1980s, the partnership has completed over two hundred projects, with a particular emphasis on housing and low-cost industrial buildings. In doing so, they have evolved an original and highly successful building type, based on compact blocks with central access, an inner ring of services, an outer one of variously laid-out rooms and perhaps most distinctively of all, an external semi-public layer of loggias and balconies which are enclosed by a fixed or moveable skin consisting of timber slats or sliding elements. These abstract volumes with their shutters and louvres are a modern interpretation of the massive old houses of the Rhine Valley and the Vorarlberg region.

In 1998, following on from an earlier commission for a timber merchant in Bavaria, Baumschlager and Eberle were asked to design a wood warehouse and workshop in the southern German town of Böhen. The two-storey building occupies a gently sloping site in an isolated location near some houses and industrial premises. The architects took advantage of the topography by sinking the basement storage level into the hillside. The upper workshop floor is conceived as a long rectilinear volume, its mass softened by an external skin of vertically aligned larchwood slats. The visible sides of the lower storey are clad in translucent glass, so that the slatted timber box appears to be hovering above the ground. Both end walls are fully glazed.

On the long west elevation, the larch slats are interrupted by panels of japanned steel, into which is set a small doorway, almost domestic in scale, giving access to the workshop. The entrance is connected to a simply detailed, external concrete staircase with a slim metal balustrade that leads down to the storage level below. Materials are deployed with skill and sensitivity and the opaque solidity of the steel contrasts with the lightness of the larch slats. At night, the entire building pulsates with light, through a glazed inner wall behind the timber skin, giving a tantalizing glimpse of its interior life.

right *A simple concrete stair with a steel balustrade leads up to the elevated door that provides access to the workshop. The door is, in fact, set within a massive set of double sliding doors that allow large pieces of timber to be loaded in and out of the building.*

Exterior elevation

above *The double sliding doors take up nearly a third of the entire long elevation of the box-like building.*

left *At the short end of the building, a thick frame and a recessed glazed wall overlooking the protruding deck emphasizes the idea of the construction as a timber box.*

ALVARO SÍZA
SANTA MARIA CHURCH, MARCO DE CANAVEZES, PORTUGAL, 1997

Alvaro Síza's new Catholic church in the small Portuguese town of Marco de Canavezes joins the growing number of contemporary ecclesiastical buildings that powerfully express a sense of the spiritual in the everyday. Housing a church and mortuary chapel, Síza's exquisitely austere building forms the first part of a new parish complex for the expanding town. A community centre and parish residence will eventually be added, organized around a new plaza at the church's west end. Funding for the project has come equally from the European Union, local government and the religious community.

Perched high on a ridge above the River Douro, Marco de Canavezes lies some 30km (18.5 miles) east of Porto, Portugal's second city, where Síza lives and works. Elevated around 4m (13ft) above the level of the road, the plateau-like site has extensive views across the Douro valley to the south and west. Síza's design exploits the topography by placing the mortuary chapel at the lower road level, with the main volume of the church above. Wrapped in a rough-hewn carapace of local granite, the mortuary chapel forms a rusticated base, or plinth, for the surgically white stucco box of the church. The plinth incorporates a broad external staircase that winds up through a cloistered courtyard beside the mortuary chapel, creating a promenade to the entrance plaza of the church.

The singular white volume of the church is articulated by the barest handful of incidents. A narrow strip of horizontal glazing is incised into the long flank of the south wall, like a long visor and the gently curving north wall is punctuated by three large clerestory windows. A ceremonial doorway, 10m (32ft) tall, dominates the main west elevation. On Sundays and feast days, the massive, wooden panelled doors are thrown open, filling the soaring volume of the nave with people and sunlight. The doors are flanked by a pair of rectangular towers. One tower houses a side door for everyday use and an internal staircase that leads to the organ and belfry; the other forms a huge lightwell over the baptistry. On the east front, the elevation is divided into three bays with inward-curving corners, a subtle distillation of traditional form, but this time with stark geometry and an absence of applied decoration. The church in Marco de Canavezes appears to be the antithesis of Portugal's lavish, visceral Baroque Catholic churches. Instead of images and ornamentation, Síza harnesses the essential materiality of form and play of light to evoke a powerful sense of the numinous.

left *The tall, improbably proportioned timber doors dominate the church, with its almost uninterrupted smooth white walls.*

169

left *With the doors open, sunlight streams into the dim interior, creating a directional focus towards the liturgical east end of the chapel.*

above left *Two towers flank the entry doors, one containing the belfry and the other the baptistry.*

above right *The bells, high up in the tower, are contained within a simple white frame, in keeping with the simplicity of the rest of the building's architecture.*

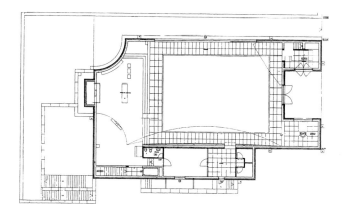

Floor plan

INDEX

ACKNOWLEDGMENTS

Author's Acknowledgments
Thanks are due to all the architectural practices who contributed information and material for this book. Thanks should also go to my colleagues on *The Architectural Review*, and the editorial team at Mitchell Beazley for their support and patience.

Photographic Credits
Key: **b** = bottom; **c** = centre; **l** = left; **r** = right; **t** = top

AKG, London: **6-7**, **12**, **12-13** t

Tadao Ando Architect & Associates: **130** tl, **130** tr, **130** c, **130-131**, Mitsuo Matsuoka: **19**, Hiroshi Ueda **131**.

Arcaid/Richard Bryant/ Architect: Richard Rogers Partnership **155** tl; Architects: Stirling and Wilford **18**; David Churchill/Architect: Alfred Waterhouse **14**; Paul Raftery/Architect: Frank Gehry **63**; Natalie Tepper **11**

Arcblue.com/Peter Durant/Architect: John Winter **156** t;

Archipress/Architect: Christophe Lab **36** tl, **37**, Franck Eustache/Architect: Francis Soler **48**, **49** tr, Michel Moch/Architect: Oscar Niemeyer **90**, **91**

Architecture Studio: **140**, **143** r;

Arquitectonica **60** t, Paul Maurer **60** cr, **61**

Farshid Assassi, Assassi Productions/Architect: Herbert Lewis Kruse Blunck: **42** t, **43**

Baumschlager & Eberle: **165**, **166** b, **166-167**, **167** b

L & E Beaudouin: **84** b r, **85**, Jean Marie Monthiers **84** b l

Will Bruder: **92** tl, **92** b, **93**

Alberto Campo Baeza: **59** r

Martin Charles/Architect: Richard Rogers Partnership **153**, **154**, Architects: John Winter **157**

Corbis UK Ltd: **8**, **9**

Daly Genik: **29**, **30** tr, Iris Schneider **30** tl

Richard Davies/Architect/Future Systems: Front jacket, **32**, **33**, **106-107**, **108-109**, **109** t

Design Antenna **95** t;

Diller and Scofidio: **116** t

Edifice/Darley/Design: Ian Schrager/Philippe Starck/Architect: Harper Mackay: **123**

Engelen Moore: **22**

Luis Ferréira Alves/Architect: Eduardo Souto de Moura: **118-119**, **120**, **121** tl, **121** tr

FMGB Guggenheim Bilbao/Erika Barahona Ede: **64** t, **64-65**

Foster and Partners: **39** tl, **39** b, **40**, **103** b, Nigel Young **103** tr

Future Systems: **32** b, **109** b

Frank Gehry: **64** b

Gigon Guyer: **96** b

Roland Halbe/Architect/Enric Miralles and Benedetta Tagliabue: **161** tr

Harper Mackay: **122**

Jörg Hempel Photodesign/Architect: Hadi Teherani: **112-113**, **114** tl, **114** tr

Herbert Lewis Kruse Blunck: **41** b

Herzog and De Meuron: **125** b

Ross Honeysett/ Architects:Engelen Moore: **23**, **24**, **25** tl, **25**

Steven Holl: **74** b

Carl-Viggo Hølmebakk: **144** b, **146** tl, **146** tr, **146** b, **147**, Jiri Havran **144-145**

The Interior Archive/Cecilia Innes/Architect: Yturbe: Back cover

Japan Architect Co. Ltd/Shinkenchiku-Sha/Architect: Kazuyo

Sejima: **98-99**, **99** b; Architect: Kengo Kuma: **27**

Katsuhisa Kida/Architect: Ushida Findlay: **44** tl, **44-45**, **46** tr, **47**

Kengo Kuma: **26**, **26-27**

Christophe Lab: **36** b

John Linden/Esto Photographics/Architect: John Pawson **111** t

Duccio Malagamba/Architect: Enric Miralles & Benedetta Tagliabue: **158-159**, **160**, **161** tl, Architect: Alvaro Siza **170**, **171** tl

John Mansell: **156** b

Marks Barfield :**76**

Mecanoo: **81** b

Enric Miralles & Benedetta Tagliabue: **161** b

Michael Moran/Architect: Williams Tsien: **51**, **52**, **53** l, Architect: Diller & Scofidio: **116** b, **117**

Jacques Moussafir: **34**, **35** l, **35** r

Neutelings Reidijk: **139** t

Oscar Niemeyer: **91** b

Jean Nouvel: **70** b

Juhani Pallasmaa/Gérard Dufresne: **82**, **83**, **83** b l

John Pawson: **54** b, **110**

Undine Prohl/Architects: Daly Genik **28**, **31**

Helmut Richter: **148**, **150** tl, **150** tr, **150** b, **151**

Christian Richters/Architects: Herzog de Meuron **124**, **125** t, Architect: Mecanoo **80**, **80-81**, Architect: Alvaro Siza: **168-169**, **171** tr, Architects: Van Berkel & Bos **131** t, **132**, Architect: Erik Van Egeraat **162** t, **163**

Richard Rogers Partnership: **152**

Kazuyo Sejima: **98** b

Alvaro Siza: **171** b

Francis Soler: **49** b

Eduardo Souto de Moura: **119** b, **121** tr

Studio Granda: **87**

Hisao Suzuki/Architects: Alberto Campo Baeza: **58** b, **58-59**

Hadi Teherani: **114** b, **115**

Tom Turner: **10**

Ushida Findlay: **46** b

Van Berkel & Bos: **133** b

Herman H. van Doorn Gkf/Architects: Neutelings Reidijk: **138**, **139** b

Erik Van Egeraat Associated Architects: **162** b

View/Philip Bier/Foster & Partners: **38-39**, **39** tr ; Architect: Frank Gehry **62**; Peter Cook/Architect: Le Corbusier **16**; Architect: Richard Rogers **155** tr, Architect: Scott Tallon Walker **126-127**; Chris Gascoigne/ Architect: Fletcher Priest **5**, Dennis Gilbert/ Architect: Design Antenna **94**, **95** c, Architect: Foster & Partners **101**, **102**, **103** tl, Architect: Studio E **56-57**, Architect: Studio Granda **86**, **88** tl, **88** tr, **89**, Architect: Studio Granda with Kristin E Hrafnsson **20-21**, Architect: Weston Williamson **104-105**; Richard Glover/Architect: John Pawson **111** b, **54-55**, **55**, Peter MacKinven/Architect: Alvaro Siza **2**, Paul Rafferty/Architect: Jean Nouvel **68-69**, **70** tl, **70** tr, **71**, Nathan Willock/Architect: Rietveld **17**

Von Gerkan Mark: **72** t, **72** b, **73**

Paul Warchol Photography Inc/Architect: Stephen Holl **74-75**, **75** t, **135**, **136**, **139** tl, **139** lr

Gaston Wicki/Architect: Architecture Studio: **141**, **142**, **143** l, Architect: Gigon Guyer : **96-97**, **97**

John Winter and Associates: **156** b

Nick Wood Photography/Architects: Marks Barfield **77**, **78**, **79** tl, **79** tr